Your Neighborhood of Poems

© 1994
All Rights Reserved
Printed in the United States of America
First Edition
First Printing

Editors: Eloise Bradley Fink, John Dickson
Cover Art: Peggy Shearn

A grant from the Illinois Arts Council has contributed to this project. Thorntree Press, a not-for-profit publisher, acknowledges contributions from friends whose tax-deductible gifts helped to make this book possible.

ISBN (Paperback)   0-939395-45-2
Library of Congress Catalog Number: 94-060897

Published in 1994
Thorntree Press
547 Hawthorn Lane
Winnetka, IL 60093

Table of Contents

PHIL ALEXANDER
- The New Phase 9
- Season Strategies 10
- Electronic Voices 10
- Triage 11

DOLPH ANDREWS
- The Empire Gold Mine—Cornwall 13

JOHN J. BALLENGER
- You Understood and I Think I Did Too 14
- Cross Country Skiing 15

KAREN E. BEARDSLEE
- Grandma 16
- Woolly Worms 16

TERRI BERNSOHN
- Our Theory of Marriage 18

RICHARD E. CARTER
- Revisiting An Old Teacher 19
- The Red Airplane 19

JOHN DICKSON
- Driving to Hillcrest 22
- Layover 23
- Chagall 24

CAROL DINE
- Two Gods 26

BEVERLY DRICK
- Transition 27
- Assignment 27
- Will, Codicil Number One 28

SUSAN V. FACKNITZ
- The Limits of Love 29

NANCY CARLIN FIGEL
- Connect the Dots 30
- Back Home 32
- On the Irish Side of Heaven 32
- Leave Taking 34

ELOISE BRADLEY FINK
- Like Going Home 35
- Touristing Alaska 36

JANICE FINNEY
- Hanging Laundry: A Ritual 37
- Headcount 37
- Arrival 38

CYNTHIA GALLAHER
- Gulf Sheep 40
- Penguins 41

PATRICIA GANGAS
- Rain 42
- Technology 43
- Dark Days 45

BRUCE J. HARRIS
- A Country Woman, City Streets 46
- The Back Window 47

PHILIP HEETER
- Where the Swing Set Used To Be 48
- Signal Fire 50

B. F. HELMAN
- Autumn 51

BILL HENNESSEY
- In Indian Land 53
- All This Trouble 53

BECCA HENSLEY
- Old Lady With a Broom 54

HY HIRSHFIELD
- Saturday Movies 56
- Principles Forever 57
- Write, Write, Write 57
- Poetic Impasse 58

ADRIENNE HOCHSTADT
- The Curmudgeon Man 59

BARBARA SAVADGE HORTON
- Last Night 60

GORDON HOWARD
- For Eleanor 61

LINNEA JOHNSON
- Night on the Rio Grande 62
- Belief 63

DAVID JONES
- The Widow's Red Canoe 64
- Two More Legs 65

ROBERT JONES
　Front Porch at Home 66
MARYANN GALVIN KOFOED
　Cicadas in Motion 67
PETER J. LAFORGE
　Once 67
JOHN LINDBERG
　Gardening Naked in the Rain..68
　Mulberry Leaves 69
ROBERT LINDNER
　Anne, Age Sixteen 69
　Kiss at the Black Canyon 70
　Grand Mesa Lupine 71
　Baboon Organ Transplant...72
BRUCE LOEWENTHAL
　Bird 2 73
KATHLEEN B. MADDOX
　The Lake 74
CHRIS MANDELL
　In the Nursing Home 74
　The Homeless 75
　A Night Together on the Beach 75
SHERRI LEDERMAN MANDELL
　After Birth 76
　Peacocks 76
　Riding 77
ROBERT MC CRAY
　Poetic Justice 78
COLLEEN MC MANUS
　Gone 79
KAT MEADS
　Reckoning 81
HARRIET J. MELROSE
　It Only Happened Once 81
JESSE MILLNER
　My Back Roads 83
　Outdoor Cafe Distances..84
　Bottomland Song 85
　What Frightens Me 85
ROBERT MILLS
　A Gaggle of Poems Almost in Flight 86
　Unanswered Dialogue...87

EDWARD MORIN
    Sylvia Skiing 88
LOUELLEN MURRAY
    Mutations 89
ALLISON J. NICHOL
    Cancer Scare 90
    San Antonio Stroll 91
    Original Sin 92
B. Z. NIDITCH
    Death Squads 92
MOIRA NOLAN
    Life Starts at Fifty 94
ALICE OLDS-ELLINGSON
    Childhood 95
    After the Doctor Tells Me I'm Dying 96
JOAN POLIKOFF
    To Nadia Comaneci 97
    Before You Leave 97
    My Cousin's Lover Dies from AIDS 98
HELEN G. REED
    Her Husband's Deaths 99
    Like Love 100
    Women's Bodies 100
    Daring 101
ANTHONY RIPLEY
    Autumn Love Song 102
    Confessions of a Pallbearer 103
    Moths 104
    The Bureaucrat Works Late 106
RUTH ROMANENGHI
    I Cry at Comedies 108
MARYANN BENNETT ROSBERG
    May 1: Beltane 109
    Back to Thunderlings 110
    Cat Annie 111
    In the Lapwing of Thought 112
    Snow, Going Home 113
JOAN Z. ROUGH
    August Observed 114
CHARLOTTE ROYAL
    Train to Toulon 116
    Anastacia 117

SARAH RUHL
- The Evolution of the Kiss 118
- The Evolution of a Phrase Close to Dying......................119
- The Glad Animal Movements All Gone By 120
- Cancer of the Mouth 121

NATALIE SAFIR
- Words for White 123

ROBERT SAWYER
- The Country Boy 123

DON SHEARN
- Thaw 124
- Lunch in Chinatown 125
- The Spring Tour: Dubuque 126

PEARL B. SHERIDAN
- Not Always Ambivalent...127
- Two Boys in Gray, Two Boys in Blue 128

KAREN KOWALSKI SINGER
- It's Beginning to Look Like Christmas at the Diner 129

MARY WREN SMALL
- Grandma 130
- The Journey Back 131
- On Being Old 131

CHRISTINA SMITH
- Vista 132

MICHAEL S. SMITH
- Jumping for Joy 133

MARILEE SNYDER
- Migraine Love Poem Above a Construction Site 135

CAROL SPELIUS
- Poets' Round Robin at Conference 136

HEIDY ANNE STEIDLMAYER
- The Healer 137

CAROLINE M. TONSOR
- August..138
- Waterdays 138

MEMYE CURTIS TUCKER
- Anna Leaves Her Radio On 139
- Rubato 140

ROD TULLIS
- A Destination 140

CONSTANCE M. UTLEY
- Christmas Card...142

WENDY WACKER
    A Marriage 143
CHERYL WALDSTEIN
    Last Gifts 144
    Ruth Rose 146
JUNE M. F. WILDEMAN
    To Drink a Star 147
    When I Was a Child 147
RICHARD ZABRANSKY
    The Night Father Cried 148
    Dolls 149
    My Wife's Cousin Mary Calls From the Bronx 150

PHIL ALEXANDER

THE NEW PHASE

My first day as a retiree,
I dig in thin topsoil
and muscular clay to re-set
eight mossy bricks in my garden.
A summer breeze hardens dirt
in my fingernails as pink on top
as when I dug out trees
for pay fifty years ago.

What next, I wonder,
my pampered days now ended?
Follow my gray colleague
to the White Mountains?
Days he carves like savory
roasts into two-hour slices—
writing, Shakespeare,
cello in a string quartet,
testing his new heartflows
in birdwalks with his wife
on his "private trail'
through parkland hardwoods.

His letters radiate light,
as if New Hampshire
had no nights...Do I go?
I don't know.

I stamp on the implanted bricks.
They're bonded to their mates
like a well-made bridge
hooked to natural teeth,
spanning extracted incisors.
No dentist could have done better.

SEASON STRATEGIES

New treatment dates set,
I leave the cancer center
with good results
and drive north from Evanston,
a late April snow on the ground,
the lake gray in the early sun.

I think of Valdesso,
general to Charles V,
body purple-streaked
from sword cuts.
Wars and duels
had been his life
for forty years
when he lay down his sword,
so "time might exist
between the life of a soldier
and his death."
He lasted seven years,
a weaver of baskets
in a monastery near Seville.

Valdesso would tell me
to stop the car,
to watch the light on the water,
to feel for blossoms
beneath the snow.

ELECTRONIC VOICES

"Decision to be made tonight,
will call you either way tomorrow."
...Voice mail from my would-be boss,
an athlete my son's age, his eyes
quiet and green as he sized me up,
last words—"like you, back
to you soon."

At dawn I record a new greeting,
twenty words, all short,
"client" used twice, "dash" once,
tone brisk yet relaxed—
juices suggested, hot and fast,
and a head more wise than gray.

At nine I find his voice
deep in the mailbox—
number three of four—
"fully qualified...
couldn't say yes to two people...
nothing to do with age...
offer went to a man
experienced in Tokyo
markets...sure you'll understand."

When my wave was at crest
my lies were as bad—delivery much worse.
But when I cut down hopefuls
I had to listen
to their cracked voices
as they said thank you
and hung up.

TRIAGE

They fill up a file rack
wide as a child's desk—
drafts from 20 years of poetry class.
Re-reading the marked-up copies
I hear dead friends—
Barry, Grace, Francis.
Later, Neurine cheers me on
behind her scrawl—"This goes
on my refrigerator...Why
so long to see the real you?"

She was right, of course.
The core of my onion—

its good clean stench—
mostly is buried beneath
layers of yellow skin.

Duplicates go into the blue
recycling bin first,
next fictions with heroes
I can't forget or understand:
the carrier pilot
sketching his wife in chalk
an hour before flak killed him,
the saint with a Winnetka income,
the sailor on a Brooklyn pier,
the young woman beside him
tense in a green rainslick.

Now and then what's written
has the stink of truth:
the cancer cell a chess player
smiling toward his next move,
the incision in Ann's skull
white against her Florida tan,
father's laughter as he tossed
my college gear onto the train
a month before he died,
the children as babies
pink in Ann's arms.

The bin is full now.
One manila folder stands in the file rack,
smelling of kitchens.

Phil Alexander *began writing poetry 20 years ago to see if he could.*

"Once in a while a poem comes out almost perfect at the first try. Those are gifts—cherish them!—and they make up for all the re-writing normally demanded." —*Lucia Getsi*

DOLPH ANDREWS

THE EMPIRE GOLD MINE—CORNWALL

In the framed 1882 picture on the wall
Snapped one or two minutes before their shift,
They stare;

Thirty of them
From fourteen to fifty-four-years-old
Sit one behind the other in the mine car,
Hold tin pails of soup and biscuits,
Anticipate ducking
Their heads under the beams
Hurtling into the dark
To the water pumps' thudding.
The next group,
Pails in hand,
Waiting their turn.
Twenty mules pulled the ore
Back and forth,
Never leaving the mine.

Two hundred yards from the mine's entrance,
Dominating the knoll, the owner's four-story house.
Its two-terraced gardens surround it.
He used the mansion either one spring month
Or three weeks in the fall.
Late for the tour,
We look through
The triangular glass window.
The oak table
Reflecting the chandelier,
A porcelain serving bowl.

We walk back to the parking lot.
Invisible and silent
Beyond the cone-full pines,
The miles of flooded tunnels and shafts.

Dolph Andrews thinks of poetry sometimes when his daughter is eating oatmeal.

"I labor by singing lights/Not for ambition or bread/But for the common wages/of their most secret heart." —*Dylan Thomas*

JOHN J. BALLENGER

YOU UNDERSTOOD AND I THINK I DID TOO

It was a gift, those last days,
out of danger, we said,
out of the hospital,
in the sunlight,
without pain
but you understood,
I did, too

The circle of time
was curling back,
approaching slowly
on padded feet.
Later, in the hospital again,
suspecting this was the last,
I wanted, without discouraging,
to ask for one last word
but dared not do so.

Having done the possible,
the doctor was busy with others
whose battle was still ebb and flow.
You understood
and I think I did, too.

It was the nurses,
in and out,
cheerfully
tucking in the sheets,

placing a pillow between the knees
who were the guardians
the confreres, the elixir
to ease you and me,
like guiding blindness,
over the stile and down the walk
to the field beyond.

CROSS COUNTRY SKIING

Nodding, drifting
close to sleep
with lub dub beats
metallic slosh of skis
on cracking snow.
I'm nearly hypnotized
by leaden slaps
as poles are pushed
and pushed again
to fracture
rippled crusts of frost.

I'm unaware of pulses surging
in head and chest.
My skis make songs
to lead me on.

I race whiteness,
not to win,
but just to stroke the drifts,
and cut the path,
to echo distance,
swallow space,
to freeze the wind,
and fire my cheeks.
I hold my edge,
and stay the course.

Propped on a tree,
my skis at rest,

I scoop the air
up from my lungs.
It floats away.

John J. Ballenger, M.D., after a life time of practicing medicine and keeping current a text, <u>Diseases of the Nose, Throat, Ear, Head and Neck</u>, now happily indulges himself in the practice of—as poet physician William Carlos Williams said—"word-smithery."

"If Galileo had said in verse that the world moved, the Inquisition might have left him alone." —Thomas Hardy

KAREN E. BEARDSLEE

GRANDMA

Her smell,
like hot molasses,
moves on the air in waves
as thick as dust storms.
When I am near her,
Saliva seeps from the deep of my mind and mouth.
I can taste her smell,
fresh and fire on the tongue.
Held there, just for a moment,
before letting it seep slowly,
slowly, down the throat and over
the cool areas that wait so long in anticipation
of the warmth.
Wait, to be covered and soothed
with a liquid
that is lighter than gold
and darker than moonlight.

WOOLLY WORMS

On the phone with you, Mom,
I realized that at this point
in your life—I mean—

when you were my age,
24 almost 25,
you carried a girl on each hip,
had a home in Connecticut
and a husband at work.
Me, on the other hand,
24 going on 25,
I still have a bookbag,
a one-bedroom apartment
and a dog.
You said my sister
told you the other day
you were getting old.
Do you still remember
pocketsful of woolly
worms from the woods in the back yard?
Spread out on the kitchen
table. All of them
and us wrapped
in warm winter jackets.
And you explaining
which ones would predict
and survive
the winter ahead.
I wonder, Mom—
that is, I wanted
to ask you,
Mom,
Are you—I mean—
are we
getting old?

Karen E. Beardslee, *a graduate student and adjunct professor, finds story ideas and poem pieces everywhere. It is what she does to make her life all come together.*

"Poetry uses words, images, motions and rhythms to come to a kind of dumbfounding. It comes to the things that have been focused and you have simply reached the unspeakable." —from an interview with A. R. Ammons

TERRI BERNSOHN

OUR THEORY OF MARRIAGE

When you asked if I like to go skiing,
I thought that I answered quite clearly...
But what you thought I meant (if I might be so bold)
Is I like to be out in the sub-freezing cold,
Getting jostled and poked while I wait for the lifts,
Dislodging my ski-tips from 4-foot-high drifts,
Drinking boiling hot cocoa from Styrofoam cups
While my nose starts to run and my glasses steam up...
But I meant that I like it in theory.

When I asked how you felt about big families
What I heard, when you answered my query,
Was you like the hysterics, the chaos, the noise,
The mountains of laundry, the diapers, the toys;
You wouldn't mind wiping up blood, milk or tears
Or not sleeping through one whole night in 5 years,
That it wouldn't be hard to get used to the dirt,
Giving up Macneil-Lehrer for Ernie and Bert...
But you meant that you like them in theory,

So you asked if I'd like to get married
—and you know that I do love you dearly—
But I thought I'd end up with someone more funny,
While you'd like a woman who'd earn half the money,
And although money markets and stock plans are nice,
We're investing in preschool and more Fisher-Price;
And the two kids you planned on turned out to be three
(thank goodness the big one is learning to ski...)
We love to be married, in theory.

Terri Bernsohn is author of many poems and short stories, as well as one unwritten novel.

"...When love comes to me and says/What do you know, I say This girl, this boy." —Sharon Olds

RICHARD E. CARTER

REVISITING AN OLD TEACHER

Following the loon's tremolo
across a sky of layered moods
still dripping from its morning shower,
I found a sunflower-yellow
Piper Cub blooming
in a field of brooding green.

Pacing its outline,
wet grass squishing my socks,
I took in every wire,
brace, hook and pulley,
noted each curving ellipse
and long, true line,
admired layers of lacquer
on Irish linen stitched
and stretched tom-tom tight
over wooden ribs.
The shape of flight.

Tracing the wing's edge,
my finger collected suspended pearls,
restrung the coolness
down the inside of my bare arm
and remembered how
she once taught me
the sky dance.

THE RED AIRPLANE

I wish I could write
my brother, Robert,
tell him,
"I saw a red Aeronca
on skis
headed north today."
He would have known....

He would have seen
two men side by side
squeezed into a tight cockpit,
stuffed into blaze-orange parkas
flying over a fresh snowscape
sharing something few men know.

He would have seen
a coffee thermos jammed between them,
the man on the right holding
a steaming, sweet smelling cup
for both of them,
chart folded on his lap.
The man on the left with a thick-mittened
grip on the stick,
both grinning,
their lips rolled up high
like they would never
come down.

They fly away
like kids who sneaked out of school
and got away clean,
giddy, going no place special
just going, cold toes and all.
The scroll of earth unwinds
in measured time below
cranking out Christmas card barns
and a snow subdued land
splashed with rice paper lakes
colonized by fishing shanties

No words
Just a nudge of elbow,
nod of head,
an image shared,
perhaps the ice tracings
like the tracks of figure skaters
going over and over a move...
ice boats
on Geneva's frozen green,
their sails as swift as shark's fins.

Somewhere in the unmarked whiteness,
they would land,
maybe on a lake
to surprise a fisherman
hunched over a hole
line in hand,
or at a snow-drowned airport
waiting for the plows.

So many choices.
All of them theirs.
No control tower
just the red Aeronca,
the sky,
the slanted light,
and the two of them
flying side by side,
characters painted
into the scene.

When they finally land
on the purple snow
of December dusk,
they would slip down
an unseen slide,
splash in a great swoosh,
the white pluming out behind
and hiss in a glide
across unmarked snow.
Then listen to the silence
measured by
ticking of the cooling engine.
Too old to say, "Whee!"
they would let the sound
rise up in them,
and hold the day inside.

Dear Robert,
    I saw a red Aeronca
    on skis
    headed north today.
        Good-bye,
            Richard

Richard E. Carter, pilot, poet, planner, geographer, photographer, and naturalist.

"*Are you in earnest? Seize this very moment! What you can do or dream you can do, begin it. Boldness has genius, power and magic in it.*"

JOHN DICKSON

DRIVING TO HILLCREST

There comes a time, we decided,
a time, we supposed,
when some sort of action has to be taken,
some sort of decision has to be made.
After all, his age...
lost in the hallways of his mind,
the sparkle of his eyes gone dim.

Arrangements were made and few days passed,
memorable for their absence of feeling
and very little conversation.
I was chosen to do the driving
with Uncle Ben sitting beside me,
just the two of us driving to Hillcrest,
taking him to the nursing home.

His daughters helped him into the car,
wrapped the piano shawl over his shoulders,
his old turtle eyes imbedded in wrinkles.
He was quiet as we drove away,
as we passed through familiar neighborhoods
and city streets with their towering buildings.
A helicopter hovered above.

But all the while I kept thinking of Ben
until he became Chief Wild Calf
or maybe old Chief Eagle's Feather,

his face of stone and his eyes in the distance,
wrapped in furs and led by the women
to his old canoe near the mouth of the river.
They tucked him in gently and set him adrift
for his ride to the open sea,
past well-worn trails and familiar trees.
The towering cliffs on either side
framed the horizon of sea and sky
reminding me of the entrance to Hillcrest.
A grey hawk hovered
leading the way to eternity.

Then gradually Ben became Ben again,
waiting patiently for the end of his future,
as stoic as old Chief What's-His-Name.
It was then I figured to hell with Hillcrest
and drove down some side roads that led back home.

LAYOVER

Someone in Knoxville looks like me—
nothing phenomenal...after all,
how many versions of human face can there be?
Like snowflakes, perhaps, but even so,
who can say there are no two alike?
Who has photographed every snowflake?
Or every human face?

Three times I've taken the southbound bus—
always different, but always the same.
It reaches Knoxville around about midnight,
weaves through streets of snoring houses,
veers through poorly-lighted alleys,
then rests dark and dormant 'til six in the morning
while I wait in the waiting room, wait in limbo
until just before the sun comes up.

Each time as I wait there, part of the bench,
someone jolts me alive, always calling me Bob.
"Bob! Bob! Where have you been?
Just yesterday we were talking about you.
How's your daddy since Martha died?"

Who was this first one, this creaky old man
with the stiff octogenarian joints?
And who was Martha? Who was Bob?
I gave him a smile of recalling old times
and drifted back to my foggy condition.

A year or two later it happened again.
A youngish woman sat next to me
saying, "Oh, Bob—we missed you tonight.
What a wonderful party...you should have come.
Did you stay away because of Ruth?
Was that the reason? Was it? Was it?
Forget her, Bob—she isn't worth it."
Who was this woman? And who was Ruth?
I told her I hadn't seen much of Ruth.
"Don't lie to me, Bob...you were thick as thieves.
And don't talk like a stupid yankee!"
She walked off and boarded the Crossville bus.

A few months ago it was three men—
authority figures in business suits.
One woke me with a nudge in the shins.
"What are you up to this time, Bob,
loitering in this deserted station?
If you value your job, get to work on time.
No more of this nonsense from now on."

If I ever get tired of being me
I may go to Knoxville and start being Bob,
do a few good deeds to patch up his image
or talk with a drawl and look up Ruth.
Or if it turns out he's died by then,
I'll be Bob freshly returned from the grave
and maybe set off a whole new era.
After all, what's life without some sort of mission?

CHAGALL

Born in a little Russian village
where all the houses were topsy-turvy—

even the heads of some of the people
were upside down or completely detached.
Born with an urge to praise God
by painting everything he saw,
even dragging his childhood through life
and painting it over and over and over
with a mixture of color and homesick tears—
the horse and wagon in the air
drifting past his open window
as a fiddler sits on the neighbor's chimney
putting the day to music.

Lovers in green...lovers in blue...
lovers with wrinkles and years on their faces.
Lovers on a donkey's back
or the moon a crescent in the sky
as the lovers float above the town,
as a bridesmaid drifts in through the window.
"Art," he said, "is a state of mind."

The Bible so much a part of his life
he thought Jacob and Isaac lived down the road
and he wouldn't have been a bit surprised
if Goliath came looming over the hill.

His village of animals and people,
all sharing the same sad ending.
Talk to the cow...confide in the cow...
on cold mornings milking the steaming cow...
watching his grandfather slaughter the cow...
refusing, but finally eating the cow,
then forever the cow being part of him.

Chagall...Chagall...I saw him once
as he watched the workmen build his mosaic
by the Dearborn side of the First National Bank.
Maybe he saw me. Maybe not.
Maybe he even painted my picture
wearing my suit and a horse's head.
Or maybe floating slightly above him
looking down on him
smiling my blessing.

John Dickson was twelve when he shop-lifted a small poetry book from a second-hand store. Since then he's been trying to repay his debt to society.

"It was years before I learned that what I was writing was poetry."
—Pablo Neruda

CAROL DINE

TWO GODS

At first, they were demigods.
Then They made birds
and learned how to listen.
They discovered stars
so They could see each other
naked in the dark.

She is my age, dressed in leaves.
She says, "Grin and bear it."
He is an old man with white hair
who lives in the sky.
He made fire and tipped the earth
like a uterus. She made a stone
so heavy He cannot lift it.

Two Gods have all the advantages—
knowing the dimensions of pain,
how to lean into it
the way a river bends.

They monopolize pleasure:
She is the kiss, the lover
and the beloved. He plays
on the harp of His bones.

Sometimes They stand in a bucket
of blood. Sometimes They pray.

Carol Dine, who tours New England as a performing artist, has a first book of poems, Naming the Sky by Golden Quill.

"...you do what you can if you can; whatever the secret, and the pain, there's a decision: to die, or to live, to go on caring about something." —Mary Oliver

BEVERLY DRICK

TRANSITION

I have been trying on old feelings
and old clothes.
Nothing fits anymore.
My body is changing;
its familiar outline is blurred, and
everyday I make a new and unsettling discovery.
I no longer recognize myself.

I'm going to the mall this afternoon
to see if I can find my body
among the hats and scarves
and dresses for sale.
Perhaps I'll discover it in a mirror,
seen unexpectedly, startling me.

I may rediscover my body somewhere
between the lingerie and the sportswear.
But where shall I shop for the rest of me?
Maybe I'll find it in a turn of phrase,
perhaps hiding in a poem.

ASSIGNMENT

This paper is out of control:
notecards in the toaster,
citations among the cushions,
sentences on the floor.

Sweep it together,
reorder the parts,
staple and hand it in.
Get it out of the house!

His memory also overruns my life.
If left to roam at will,
he catches me, unaware and breathless.
He, too, must be gathered up
and made sense of—
chaptered and labeled and footnoted:
the old lover, the last fling,
the last mistake.
Whatever it takes to get him
off the stairs,
and out of the kitchen
and onto the page,
defined and dead.

WILL, CODICIL NUMBER ONE

Tell me what you treasure
—my amethyst ring?
—a Moorcroft vase, pregnant with pomegranates?
—the Cotswold photograph overseeing my bed?

When I die it's all that will be left of me.
I have no children, no blood to run on.
Tell me where our hearts intersect
so that I may write it down.
I need to know someone will remember.

I have been trying to give myself away
in small pieces—
my green jade ring,
the shadow puppets cradled home from Bali,
the promise of a home for my tabby cat.
Some small hope of immortality in exchange
for a memento of myself.

Lately, I have been thinking
of the place I will leave vacant—

the inside of a Moore sculpture,
the openness of my light-filled home.

Perhaps I will leave a space behind.
There is comfort in that thought.

Beverly Drick *is a librarian at Oakton Community College.*

"Not by appointment do we meet Delight and Joy: They heed not our expectancy; but round some corner in the streets of life, they, on a sudden, clasp us with a smile." —Gerald Massey

SUSAN V. FACKNITZ

THE LIMITS OF LOVE
(for a friend not yet dead)

I love you, James Hughes,
and I want you back.
Not the boy I found
huddled in the corner of his rented room
under a blanket soaked with sweat and vomit.
When I lifted you to the bed
your bones felt like bird bones
you were hollowing out for flight.
Not even the man at my wedding
in tuxedo, red bow tie,
red high-tops,
who clutched my arm
tight to the bone.
Not the one who sent postcards, no return address,
who called collect from roadside phones
in trouble asking me to come.
I'll take anyone you wound up being
after the fits and the frozen hours.
When a stranger at a party
spoke the name of your last lover,
all of these came back to me.

But I want you now,
whatever has happened to the tilt
of your head, the lashes of a girl
above dark eyes, the way, once,
you lifted my face as I lowered my eyes
and all I could see
were the bones of your hand,
of my hand,
warm blood between us
in the perfect inner light
you followed too far.
I want to tell you
of the bones that broke inside of me
since that, of how it feels to heal.
And I know I cannot lift you from the floor,
but I want to feel against my hand
the firm flesh of your palm,
the warmth of your cheek
flushed with whatever has come.
Send a card
of the hipbone of a canary.
Wish yourself home.

Susan V. Facknitz *teaches creative writing and poetry at James Madison University in Virginia, where she lives with her husband, writer Mark Facknitz, and three children.*

"bringing the entire life/to this moment/the small waves bringing themselves to white paper/something like light stands up and is alive." —Muriel Rukeyser

NANCY CARLIN FIGEL

CONNECT THE DOTS

Florida—
    A dot to dot
picture

At night
From the airplane window.

Connect
    200 dots,
and the Bath and Tennis Club
    towers,
        its turrets like castle outposts,
guard against the non-members.

Connect
    1500 dots,
and the outline of Singer Island,
    beer can island,
a thousand moon-filled boating
nights ago.

Connect
    the dots
with memories
of sailing through the surf
out to the warmer Gulfstream
off to Bimini.
Or a no-name place,
Australian pines growing,
with fresh water below the coral rock line
and conch shells to
drink from.
Or coconuts.

It's only a dot-to-dot
picture now,
a landscape
mapped on graph paper
from two thousand feet,
someplace I go to
connect
dot to dot pictures
out the airplane window.

BACK HOME

His wife comes home,
alone.
But his things call out
to her.
His cane,
a walker left
in his closet.

The paraphernalia
of sickness.
A seat for the bathtub,
a bedpan,
and a hospital bed
that bends in 24 positions.

Pill bottles
row after row,
yellow and red,
bumble bee striped.

Holy cards,
miniature St. Jude prayer books,
rosary beads,
coiled black snake,
talisman
to ward off death.

A house of vigil,
when only the dog
still waits
for his return,
and his special bedtime treat,
the biscuit
that his master will give him,
the only thing on his mind.

ON THE IRISH SIDE OF HEAVEN

There he sits,
Don O'Malley does,

on that emerald side,
that green so grass side,
among the mumbling and the
muttering.

A stout in hand,
stories flowing
like the tap
in his practiced hand.

A muttering next
to him,
the lilt so familiar,
'tis Uncle Jim.
Still planing a table,
plumbing a line,
talking to hisself
about Aunt Mary's arthritis,
how he lowered the picture window,
so she could see out in her wheelchair.

And Don,
master of games, gets the poker hands going,
starts the horse talk,
and the heavenly jockeys favored.
When the chips run low,
and the table dissipates,
and his only partner
a deck of cards,
he calls to Uncle John,
the one who lost his arm
on a bet, the train roaring
down the track faster than he,
a better golfer one-handed
than most with two,
and gets serious,
a game of gin or two.

They play to the death,
until the cards grow limp,
their game faces intact,
until the final hand.

LEAVE TAKING

I see my father-in-law slipping away,
thirty pounds lighter,
his legs barely thick
as the walker's frame,
a slow shambling gait—
shuffle, pause, slide,
shuffle, pause, slide.
His whole world slipping
into the space of bedroom,
bathroom, and living room couch.
Doors to card parties
close softly.
No more bridge marathons
at church with correct
little contracts on the corners
of starched card tables.
No more loud, sawdust-covered floors
games of gin in knotty pine booths.
No more studied poker hands
at the polished oak table
with initialed glasses
filled with highballs.

The church doors
no longer friendly.
The handicapped entrance
still a handicap for him.
His daily masses,
followed by Donuts from Dollies,
no more.

He no longer huddles with
the Moose and the Elks
to sell a few policies,
to say a few words at their
next meeting on how to motivate.

No more reunions
with the class of '43,

the Fighting Irish,
and the Flying Irish.

Nancy Carlin Figel, librarian and mother of four lively children, has worked as a reporter, writer, and English teacher.

"Poetry is the dance of words; it is what's left when the music pulls away."

ELOISE BRADLEY FINK

LIKE GOING HOME

Family reunions in the rec room of the Farmer City Atom
    Power Plant, where Cousin Bob worked, seemed like going
home. The folks' farm had been there, a mile or two away—
    and Yankeetown School, up the road. The same old fork
snick-snack of chicken-and-noodles and the home-cranked
    ice cream—"Good as Gramma's," Cousin Bob had said.

This year it tasted even better while the drought had left
    their hopes all frying in the fields. Shoes scuffed soft dust.
The sun scoured miles of green away; it seemed to squat
    right down there on the prairie. Stayed. The crickets
knitted in the needle grass beside blue oiled roads—
    as "soft as Gramma's fudge, set out to cool," Bob said.

Around a pancake-shallow pond, brown ducks
    were baking in the sun like wheaty muffins.
Hunger turned rabbits so tame they came up close.
    The maples were a rattle of brown leaves, a cluster
of small fidgeting birds. The air was powder. Those big canna
    leaves, gone limp, were flopping in the wind like crows.

It was the year when round-rumped cars came back. But cattle
    were all angles; they seemed turned to bone.
They stood there like old men with no place left to go.

Bob said you couldn't find a bucket of soy beans
inside a carload. And the spindley corn leaves shuffled in uneasy
   air, next to the big blue atom tower,

anonymous as any hangman's hood, though no one said.
   Grey fields sagged up against the fence,
and no one wondered why young Bob had got a crop of cancer
   in his head, just as he'd made plant foreman.
Still, they praised the Lord for chemo and the atom power
   plant that kept them working and the high wires humming—

although next year they would meet at Rucker Chapel, bury him
   just up the road beneath the folks' chokecherry tree.

TOURISTING ALASKA

She shivers at their rubbery
   mouths like flabby canopeners.
Those sweating, mating seals
   are only giant slugs
with toe nails—squinting,
   belching, all in chorus,
like old sink drains: "Rup-erup."
   But spring brings snowy,
mewing pups, round eyes that blink
   at hunters' reddened clubs.
She reaches out to take one home,
   to keep it in her bathtub.

Eloise Bradley Fink, *although she does not see herself, as a student quipped, "the godmother of poetry," has been around a long time (public relations, texts, newspapers) reading manuscripts of writers while raising three of her own.*

When Matisse was asked if he believed in God, he said, "Only when I'm painting." I write.

JANICE FINNEY

HANGING LAUNDRY: A RITUAL

"On Mondays, we wash our clothes, wash
our clothes, wash our clothes...."

A Cambodian boy, who escaped
the Khmer Rouge, tells me of walking
with his sister in the woods.
The two discovered bodies hanging
from trees, their necks slashed, livers
sliced from bellies to be eaten.

Pride holds up his arms, crossed, to show
how each one hung, head down. His eyes
fix on the floor as if ashamed to admit
witnessing. A Buddhist, he makes
no mention of Christ but I know he knows
ritual sacrifice goads remembering.

In monotone, he describes his sister's
hysteria. Her mind cannot flee the lines
of dead ones, clothes blowing loosely
on bodies. Stunned, I try Christian
sympathy, say I understand, but the only
thing I've seen hung first-hand is laundry.

HEADCOUNT

"More than a million Cambodians died under the
Khmer Rouge from April 1975 to January 1979."
    —The New York Times

I'll tell you one.
To save bullets they used the usual,
the shovel. It rang its blunted
death-blow bell.

Into an empty cistern
she was tossed, piled with the rest
of the felled harvest. A rotten
smell woke her.

Dead rats, dogs, oxen,
she wasn't sure which. She groped
the stench, finding fingers, fingertips,
a nipple, a collage
of body parts.

Drowning, choking on stale
mouthfuls, flailing head over heels, arms
fighting legs to the surface, she pushed up
until she found the sun,
the loud blue sky
in the air.

For days she wandered, afraid
to be found alive.
A villager located her skin-and-bones
mother and a cousin, Saroeun.
Both had escaped
death's peasant hands.

The girl is living now
in Cambodia near Tonle Sap,
the large flat body of water you can find
on the map.

The still smell stays
with her and the lump on her head. All day
she sits. The smell hangs in the bright
sky, the same shoveled blue light
ringing her ears.

ARRIVAL

There is a need to keep secrets
hidden like silver, to make certain
your father's out of earshot.

Already I know the story:
the gang-rape by Thai pirates,
high waves of escape.
A stranger found your sister
washed ashore with the smell
of fish and black clouds of flies
descending on the pale yellow color
seeping from between her legs.

In the living room, you press
high-tech memory and apologize
for what did not get filmed,
a six-hour airport delay, the years
waiting. We watch your parents
land, deboard a silver 747.
They make umbrellas with their hands
to hide from the electronic sound
of English. Tongue-tied, hearing
names called, they look confused
by how quickly lives change, the
camcorder's bright florescent light.

And your father who never once broke
during eight years, the confinement
of silence, questions that felt
like beatings, this same man now
begins to cry. Streams run down
his face. He turns away, ashamed
he cannot control the release
of feeling, that he cannot stop
the yellow light from glaring, the
intrusion of the microphone shoved
toward the mouthing sounds,
the gurgling, babbling grandbaby
as she is handed close-up
to his tired wife. Speechless,
your silver mother clasps
the newborn amid a blurred whirl
of arms and shoulders embracing
the wet taste of bottled-up words.

Janice Finney, poet-playwright, is Writer-in Residence (for the Illinois Arts Council) and instructor at Truman College and Habitat for Humanity.

"*Poetry becomes as essential as bread.*" —Czeslaw Milosz

CYNTHIA GALLAHER

GULF SHEEP

"The herds mill about
because they have no pasture,
even the flocks of sheep are desolate."
       Joel 1:18

To protect us from mines,
the shepherd walks ahead
instead of trailing behind
to round up the usual stragglers,
but what tent could he pitch tonight
to cover us from the black rain?

Who could count hours
    the foul wet tongues
    wagged their fury on our coats,
not even our master who judges
days by the sun's passing,
the sun, blocked and impenetrable
as our smeared and crusted wool.

We, ancient clouds absorbing modern mistakes,
Q-tips in a misbegotten ear,
cotton balls dabbing at a prehistoric oil pan
paleolithic intentions would have kept
    underground,
even a dinosaur's rampage
would only have taken
a few of us at a time.

And though we almost slid
into oil lakes six feet deep,
and saw birds fall out of the sky,
we still could smell the earth
    beyond this desert,
    and green grass
    of the hills where we feed,
somehow, in our hunger, memory,
    or faith in the shepherd
    willing to shatter bone
    for our thick, knotty hides,
we still believed in green.

And alongside the goats, we ate deeply,
    on green hills slicked with sadness,
till the taintedness took our breaths away,
and extinguished us like fire.

PENGUINS

Your wings gave up aerial pursuits
millions of years ago,
energy-burning flights that seemed
to steady your eye
on only more and higher views of ice,
white, cold, endless,
except at water's torn edge.

Now you fly through ocean,
leaving early boatloads of smelly sailors
to think you the fish
you feed on,
your torpedo feather-for-fur oiled bodies
weaving in and out of their prolific schools
like porcelain shuttles.

It's a fluid life,
waddling on stiff spun sugar that sears the foot,
miles thick and as high from ground
as cirrus clouds,

you give yourself to salt-shocked sea
as into generous lovers' arms,
using fat, fish, and fortitude
to temper eggs into new tuxedos
on wavy palettes of cold.

Sometimes it's only you and
the frozen green algae cells
under ice
for conversation,
but your black-tie engagements
are hectic and crowded
as a New Yorker's
huddling for warmth,
vying for fish and krill
between yourselves
and the odd trawlers,
shooting like propelled missiles
for breath at the bottom
of the earth.

Cynthia Gallaher *is the author of* <u>Night Ribbons</u> *(Polar Bear Press) and* <u>Private, On Purpose</u> *(Mulberry Press).*

"I believe the best writing is the result of a fearless and never-ending scrutiny of yourself and the world."

PATRICIA GANGAS

RAIN

I remember the night you
were born, the hours of driving pain.
All those hours it rained,
a cruel rain
that kept clawing.

But you arrived complete,
a divining gift,
as your feet opened like petals,
and your fingers weaved silken threads.
I kissed your lips
hiding my joy in prayer
in that first hour,
as I stroked your ears,
soft butterflies,
and watched your eyes,
sharp blue.

But now, I walk into your
silent, strewn room
where the walls whisper your
aching absence,
grown and gone.
Your boyhood bed
stands brave against
the wheezing tramp of time.

Inside my eyes, I see
where wet trees grow
skinny twigs of memory
shooting up the dense forest
of your vining life,
And as the rain outside pounds
the whining window,
it's then
I notice that old,
sharp-pitched pain
return.
I know it will pass once more,
though all my roses have failed this year,
and spring has gone unnoticed.

TECHNOLOGY

Black butterflies
scatter the polluted,
rubbery skies...

they are like immigrant angels,
twisting in these terrible winds,
tiny creatures in flight,
For educated men,
terminal with power,
mime the art of creativity
by pressing buttons,
splitting atoms,
pouring the planet's blood
into the wet-eyed oceans—
where frightened fish dive deeper,
and the conch cries
in its uncertain home.

Science, expensive step-mother,
possessed witch,
nurses an electronic world,
drugging it to its foundations
in a jungle of
missiles,
computers,
and chemical wanderings.
Her witches' broth
inflames the ailing world
like an orchid's temper;
the earth is straining
in the stratosphere of darkness,
screeching at the curves and edges
of destruction.

O weep,
weep, world,
for our years grow skinny
we are barking like mad dogs
in our paper temples.
O listen, world,
to the children calling mama
in the botched-up cities;
listen to the old stone-eyed women
at the end of desire
who watch their gardens and the black butterflies.

"Father," they say,
"What moments are these?"
"Is there still time to regret all this?"

DARK DAYS
(for Father Dennis)

Dear friend,
does it matter that the dark days
have come—
night freezes in the air,
and dazzling sun is slung away?
The woodbirds warble, outside myself
and I hear the eternal rolling
of wandering waves.
My cries hover between memory and sound,
and their droning echoes tell me,
I am far from God,
whom I so love.

Does it matter that in this darkness
my eyes burn their bonfires
so I might see
the half-drenched face of my driven soul?
How is it, I grieve each day against the lonely sky,
for I cannot hear eternal bells
that call to me beyond the dusking earth?

Perhaps, dear friend, I have not tempered
this slate-blue will of mine
and still I wrestle daily,
huddled in the waiting eye of God.
My body, hunchbacked,
has never known the thorns
that pierce the Christ,
rumpled on His uncomplaining crucifix.
Still, this incarnate God opens up His arms
and nags me daily to relinquish all.
He asks of me to lay my dreams
beneath His saving feet,

and to surrender all,
to the furnace of His flaming heart.

So, does it matter, friend,
that your flower-kneaded soul,
gentle as some quiet candles,
could put an end to all this night,
search out the perished sun,
reshape the circlets of the wind
and wing me with wild hope towards my Beloved?
Does any of this matter?

Patricia Gangas, a former nun who has worked as an accountant, is now a wife and mother, avid tennis player, student, reader, and writer but, most of all, her "Creator's small child, who plays hop-scotch and longs for home."

"Poetry is what makes us laugh or cry or yawn, what makes our toenails twinkle, what makes us want to do this or that, or nothing."
—Dylan Thomas

BRUCE J. HARRIS

A COUNTRY WOMAN, CITY STREETS

She walks with her head steady,
chin out to the rain beating
crab grass into sidewalk cracks.
There is music in the wet crash
and she counts the meter of her

small, skirt-tight steps.
She sees mud bleed out of the cement
wounds, worms seeking shelter
from a world of dirt.
Looking up, she sees a grey

frown of sky that melted
her father to the ground.
He furrowed fields with his man-made
machines, he sprayed green leaves
with green liquid to protect them from them-

selves. He died in a wet December
slicing a pink sow belly for food,
pouring deep red into the barn floor.
Once, he said, walking on the grassy
shore line, their small dug out

of a pond rippling rings from its dark
eye, do you see the fish? A gold
fish, long like trout, bass thick
shining in shallow water.
Do they grow that big? she asked.

They can grow that big,
he said and evaporated
one night like rain drying
on slick streets, the yellow yield
of traffic lights glowing in asphalt.

THE BACK WINDOW

For sale: eighty-six Ford
Escort, new engine, whitish
"wash me" dirt, river rock smooth
tires

and a man, late twenties, tired,
minimum-wage eyes that just
smiled and lit up his leather
coat that might be
vinyl

and looks cool to the touch
of the girl, olive skin, perm-
anent curls of died mouse blond

hair bounding in rhythm to the
radio

which sings, Isn't This
The Greatest Thing? off pitch
to the girl's do you love me?
voice with a flash of the man's
teeth saying, Yes,
yes.

Bruce Harris *enjoys time with his wife Nedra, movies, and pizza with recurring themes, and is looking forward to teaching his daughter Madeline an appreciation for literature.*

"I like to think that poems are like rocks skipping water; each skip sends the imagination spontaneously in any direction until it sinks into deeper water."

PHILIP HEETER

WHERE THE SWING SET USED TO BE

My three year old daughter
named our Siamese kitten
for "Piglet," Kitlet.

I buried Kitlet out back,
beneath the redbud tree,
where the swing set used to be.

Cocoa dusted ears peaked
at full alert—ready to leap into
the fray or lick a wounded knee—

she was a territorial sort,
a one-family cat, strangers
appraised and dismissed.

Neighborhood cats
were banished into exile from
the family's sacred soil.

We moved four times
with our azure-eyed seal point.
Each was a relocation ritual.

She disappeared for days,
sometimes a week,
to stalk the new land,

to make it safe,
returning scruffed and dirty
to her now warded place.

She began to supervise me
more closely after our
three children grew up—

sitting in my lap, making
sure the grass was mowed,
warming my bed at night.

Cataracts dimmed her sight
at age eighteen; by age
twenty she could no longer

leap from floor to counter
top and refrigerator perch—
she pretended not to notice.

We dared not move chair
or table; no one
would embarrass

our small blind friend
by having her bump into
anything out of its place.

Pained by her pain,
her low mournful
howls, we had her put to sleep.

She was twenty-three. Our other
cats are loyal and lovely.
They do not spit or hiss

at Kitlet when shafts of
sunlight hint at her trailing
discreetly behind my feet

or when she rumples
the comforter on my bed
and the night is cold,

or jumps into my lap
as I doze by the fire
in my favorite chair.

They politely look away
when the late afternoon sun
reflects off her silver fur

as she sits upon her
corner of the deck,
watching me rake leaves

beneath the redbud tree,
out back, in the garden,
where the swing set used to be.

SIGNAL FIRE

I celebrate my New Year's Night sitting
beside a fire on the Lost Coast Beach—
a reaching staircase of smoke and steam
circles up into the black shrouded sky.
The driftwood fire crouches on the sand
spitting and hissing like a cornered cat.
Pacific swells hang, crash, and dissolve
at my back in front of the dark looming
mountain hole in the star-punched night.

God Hope, do you not hear me calling
over the whining and gasping surf...
kneeling beside my flaring signal fire,
burning my hopes from a receding year?

Do you not see my tiny sparks climbing
toward your distant flaming stars, crying,
"I am Here!" while the tide drowns still
another layer of churning indifference?

Can you not feel my awe at the vast-
ness of the sky and the foreverness
of the sea pounding out a symphony to
a heaven that my be bare and empty
for all its billions of match-flared stars?

In the amber-rippled firelight
lifting over the percussive water roll
and the broken shells snarling response,
I catch your whisper in my tumbed thoughts...
"I too am Here! I'm here with you."

Philip Heeter is a business consultant and is also actively involved in anything that brings him closer to nature.

"Ancient religion and modern science agree we are here to give praise, or to slightly tip the expression, to pay attention."
—*John Updike*

B. F. HELMAN

AUTUMN

If you listen closely
       today
you may almost hear the time pass.

    Seconds pouring out of clocks and watches;
      escaping from time pieces and dials;
  tumbling forward, circle after circles.
  An endless, revolving flow fleeing.
A residue of moments uncaptured,
  unattained nor embraced.

      Listen to the time
        leaking
        cascading
         avalanching from the peaks of future,
    falling into the valley of past.
Dropped from the height of eternity into its depth.
    Never recaptured; never regained;
  instantly, initially, permanently lost.
          Listen as life lives
           and leaves

     the cycles of ourselves—
    The perpetual, annual progression
      Through seasons
      Through eras
      Through time.
  Our lives orbiting in voyage round our years
     Flow constantly
       consistently
    in precise measure
repeating thoroughly, unerringly these patterned phases.
       Like the moon
         Like the planets
  In space
    In time

      In eternity.

B. F. Helman, with a B.S. in journalism from Northwestern and an M. S. in Communication, has written movie reviews and edited a newsletter, in addition to working as a radio drama producer and an actor.

"Nothing permanent ever lasts."

BILL HENNESSEY

IN INDIAN LAND

Leafy night wind
in the dogwoods
like wings lifting the
crescent moon into
your eyes,

makes a humming air
in the mountain peaks
where the shoulders
of your dress
form milk shadows.

I wonder how I got here
in Indian land
in cool adobe
in warm voices
inside a sky of stars.

You offer no answer
but an absolute reason
for not trying
to remember which road
leads back.

ALL THIS TROUBLE

What is it about you that I am
supposed to love? Is it those
2 children who replicate our behavior,
only at supernova speed,
who offer nothing in return
for the benefit of my wisdom and shelter.

Am I supposed to care that you have tolerated
my resistance to marriage and its ensuing disaster?

Should I thank you for saving my money so we could
live where there are too few trees and too many kids.
Is it important that you cultivate a garden
like a home with tender required nourishment.

Do I have to love you just because you love me?
Can't I be an old pillow reshaping myself on the
couch, stuffed in the corner, a dim light falling on a
book I'll never finish. Oh no, here you come,
spooking around each room, trying to find me and
what I need. When all I need is you,
and all this trouble.

Bill Hennessey is a high school English teacher with poems recently published in <u>Rockford Review</u>, <u>Hammers</u>, <u>Slipstream</u>, and <u>Prairie Light Review</u>.

"*Be patient that I address you in a poem, there is no other fit medium.*" —*William Carlos Williams*

BECCA HENSLEY

OLD LADY WITH A BROOM

Daily, she shuffles down the wooden steps,
her thick calves exploding
from her bruised, used flesh
like water waiting impatiently
behind a retaining wall.

With each shuffle step,
the SOULS of her cheap, sensible shoes
push flecks of green paint from the wood.
These vacuous flecks fly through the air,
uniting in ecstasy with other paint chips
from other wooden steps. They fly

in formation like butterflies
en route to Mexico for a mating ritual. As
butterflies, they frolic about the old lady's
head, forming a halo.

She is a dried papaya, not a
prune, for surely she was
the Carmen Miranda of her day.
Her teeth are gone because she used them
so greedily in consuming men, and pineapple,
and suckling pig. Now, she eats applesauce
form a baby food jar.

These days, her shape has betrayed her. First,
it was merely promiscuous and unfaithful,
loving only her, but subtly straightening her
powerful curves, filling them up with not-even-
butter-but-margarine. Then, in complete disregard
to her rituals and incantations, this old lady's
body swelled and thickened like a gangrenous thumb
or a fish that lies long dead on the beach.

Today, driven by her shoes, she reaches the
bottom step, broom in hand, and begins to sweep.
She pushes the ragged nylon bristles, back and
forth, holding the broomstick
like a wizened lover
from long ago. Together,
the lovely couple makes little piles of debris,
preserving all the patterns
of her life.

Becca Hensley *teaches at the Austin Jung Society (as well as at home with two-plus children); her poems have appeared in* <u>The New York Quarterly</u>, <u>Cape Rock</u>, <u>Nebo</u>, <u>Sulphur River Literary Review</u>, <u>Verve</u>, <u>The New Press</u>, *and* <u>Hudson Valley Review</u>.

"If I feel physically as if the top of my head were taken off, I know that is poetry." —Emily Dickinson

HY HIRSHFIELD

SATURDAY MOVIES

Here I am sitting on the curb
wondering when he'll show.
It isn't a big deal, I know,
but I'm mad, really mad,
like when he wouldn't trade baseball cards,
or took my new Schwinn bike.
Oh, it's not raining or blowing,
not uncomf'table like.
But the darn waiting, waiting's hard.
By Field's clock, 'cross the street
of the bus stop we were to meet.
Noon, he said, that's the best time.
I have money for admission,
'nuff for candy and home fare.
An extra dime for phone would help.
Maybe he forgot where.
Nah, we made the plans together.
Got to really be something!
Me, I gotta sit, do nothing,
except—yes, I can leave.
Hah! That would show him, I can bet.
'sides, I came all the way
from the West Side, by streetcar, yet,
with a whole week's allowance.

Wow! It's getting late. Will start soon.
—can go myself, I s'ppose.
Sure, that might give him a good dose
of medicine, for next time.
Five more minutes, that's all I'll wait,
then off this curb I go
and try and sneak by under twelve.
If the cashier says "no,"
what the hell, I'll pay the full price.
Everything'll be fine.
I'll see the "Bride of Frankenstein"
even if I sit alone.

PRINCIPLES FOREVER

Irving had a girl friend,
Hannah was her name.
Met each other in first grade.
Birth years were the same.

Paired together through high school,
promised they would wed
when they reached the legal age,
leastwise so they said.

Then he went to college, East
vistas new and wide.
Rich girl from New England state
determinedly he eyed.

After all, he did opine,
love may well endure,
but I'd rather marry rich.
That's my karma, sure.

WRITE, WRITE, WRITE

If your poem's reviewed
by a peer group imbued
with strong feelings adverse
to all rhyming in verse,
do not skip a heartbeat
or admit to defeat.
Just be patient; the trend
to free verse may soon end.
There are cycles, you know.
Poets tend to outgrow
current fashions and then
they appear once again.

So, the lesson to learn
is to wait for return
of the style you prefer.
It will surely recur.

Keep on plugging away,
howsoever, each day
because writing brings joy,
so be carefree; employ
any form you admire.
Hone your skill. You'll require
nothing more than desire,
for the words to inspire
you or even command
that you keep pen in hand.

POETIC IMPASSE

I want to make a statement
for all the world to know.
But I must find the right mood
to start the words to flow.

I stare hard at the ceiling,
despair grips me so tight.
Can't get my brain to unwind
or set my pen to write.

A walk about the room once,
clockwise and then again
may help me find direction,
ignite my idle pen.

But nothing seems to happen.
The spirit is not there.
I sigh a weary soul-sigh
and slump into a chair.

Now, maybe sitting down
will cancel words mundane.
The change in my position
invigorates my brain.

I'll try with a beginning
and let it make its way.

The words may find a meter,
appropriate, I pray.

Now hear me, poet peers;
critique me. I dare say,
delete a phrase, a word, a line;
do with it as you may.

But please remember I'm the one
when turnabout comes due—
that I will be the critic
for you and you and you.

Hy Hirshfield retired from medicine to write poetry and stories.

"Poetry—not a thing said but a way of saying it"—A. E. Housman

ADRIENNE HOCHSTADT

THE CURMUDGEON MAN

He blasts into the room
and breaths catch in mid-air.
We snap to attention.
The only thing fair is to scrape our chairs
To turn his way
Waiting for barbs the curmudgeon will say.

Lob one at the leader;
Lob two at the clan.
He booms, not caring if we are his fans,
Or for what has come before his arrival
For he commands our evening's survival.

His clothes a riot of colors and plaids
Scream at each other,
Not one for fads,

They shout to the cowards, I don't give a damn
For I am
The curmudgeon man.

But when he is ready and on his own time
He settles in gently to give us his rhyme
and also his prose
For he knows his own power
And he knows his own song,
This man from the past always pulls us along.

And we listen in rapture
In hope that it lasts
For curmudgeons are fading
Far into the past
As children homogenize
And blend into one
Afraid to be different
from this poet man John.

Adrienne Hochstadt, *a director of Human Resources in a Fortune 500 corporation, is a career consultant and writer who admires crones and curmudgeons.*

"We write, like Proust, to persuade ourselves that it is eternal...to transcend our life...to teach ourselves to speak with others, into the labyrinth...to expand our world...as the primitive dance their rituals. If you do not breathe through writing, then don't write."
—Diary of Anais Nin

BARBARA SAVADGE HORTON

LAST NIGHT

While you lumbered up green hills, brown bear,
while we breathed bees and honeysuckle,
last night snow fell. Our world's a paradise
of cloud we barely can believe. We're putting

two and two together, temporarily
balancing accounts. There's something in this
blue, new white-washed land that's in our blood.
You have sunk all of your breath into me
hard like climbing. I am delicately
stepping over wounds, soft places in the earth
we may fall through. You dance tender steps
around me, speak memories of what we say,
names we call to each other in the dark.
We are full of snow—that pure. You know me
surely as the prize you hold between your fingers—
grapefruit sliced with care, precision, ripe
goodness offered with the morning sun to me.

Barbara Savadge Horton has published an illustrated book, What Comes is Spring *(Knopf) and a chapbook,* The Verb To Love *(Silver Apples Press).*

"Where you were wounded, that is where your genius will be."
—Robert Bly

GORDON HOWARD

FOR ELEANOR

I like beans, buttermilk, and beer,
    pretty smiles, brown eyes,
    fine spun hair, hinting gray.
I like Chopin's Polonaise,
    the quiet of libraries.
I like silk blouses, pearl necklaces,
    the secret bloom on the face
    of a pregnant woman.
I like icicle cold martinis with olives,
    pictures of little kids
    staring at a worm.
I like writing paper,
    the feel of of a fine point pen,
    the test of argument,
    jokes in a few words.

I like serving a tennis ball,
    running around the block,
    swimming under water.
I like the smell of rain,
    smoke from a campfire,
    downy covers in a cold bedroom.
I like reaching out for you,
    the comfort of forty years,
    the touch and hold and feel.
Here's my valentine
    a poor sculpting of words
I would it were a Lladro.

    "Gordo"

Gordon Howard *is a retired dentist, pilot, and speech teacher.*

"Writing is easy. Sit in front of a typewriter and open a vein."
—Red Smith

LINNEA JOHNSON

NIGHT ON THE RIO GRANDE

In the air is the sound of insects
larger than the barn; on the ground,

men riding. The sounds chop,
pound into your nights, your bones,

into what would be sleep
but for the wind kicking heels of dirt

onto the clapboard. If you locked your doors
it would be against these men. These men

in helicopters, on horses,
ride down children into flour,
into dust, into committing themselves
to the arms of strangers,

arms of parents lost to horses, to helicopters,
to blades and hooves and noise. You tell me

of one child
over weeping that sounds like the great river,
one child boiled in night fire, hooved underwater
by these men, their noise deeper than the river
out your back door.

BELIEF

It rattles my chest to think of her singing—
notes high, round, nearly visible as bubbles
from the pipes of her throat, the "o's" of "O Holy Night"
hanging from the ribs of the tall church like a child's
interlocking paper rings hung from top tree branches
outside in cold air,
limitless sky
buoying them to sound. Her small breasts
under the choir robe the assist to the lungs enabling flight,
her thorax, abdomen, and thighs a single note. Her legs,
lutes. Her arms, belled at her throat, her mouth; her voice

gifted toward a heaven she could see into through the ribs,
the shingles, the sour red winter skies of the far south side
of Chicago grey as lead. Shale clouds. Steel mills still working
overtime then. Her voice the airborne flame of candles.

My father, disbeliever, believed
in whatever he could while she was singing; I could see
that five years old. Fifteen. Twenty-five. Singing,

her shriveled womb was strong, her failed pancreas worked,
her balled rocky finger joints flexed clean,
ache sung out of her body like spirit flung from death.
Blood few muscle, volume, push.

Through my head like summer trains she sings,
         me put to bed alone,
wheels pulling dreams through my head into the dark air
         and back again.

Any day now I expect to stretch open my mouth, hear her voice,
belief no longer necessary but song.

*Linnea Johnson is a photographer and papermaker, aching to be
able to make a living as a studio artist.*

*"Whether I am land or open water, poetry is salt marsh, where life is
profuse, filtered, and intense, and night noises are like sound
breathing."*

DAVID JONES

THE WIDOW'S RED CANOE

The widow offers me ten dollars
to paint her garage white.
With little else to do that summer
I let the job last, deliberately
stirring glistening paint
in the cool pine shade.
The widow brings iced tea
and sits on the wood pile
telling me about her husband.
When the garage is done,
another twenty for the shed,
and the widow brings out lunch.
She pretends to scold
about white paint spattered
on the bottom of her red canoe.
I don't know how it happens, exactly
that we no longer concern ourselves
primarily with paint, and the shed
takes the rest of the summer.

This afternoon, through the car window
the widow's place appears
smaller than I remembered.

The house has a new roof,
the mailbox a different name.
But on sawhorses next to the shed,
sits the red canoe, still
speckled with a young man's
carelessness.

TWO MORE LEGS

"Humans go around on two legs,
but they seem to be looking
for another pair."
      —Nereyda Garcia-Ferraz

I walk into the leg store in the Loop.
Give me, I say, those two gray furry ones,
I want to go about as a wolf,
breathing on women's necks in the subway.
I want to ride to the end of the line,
and sit on the tarry platform, howling
at the rising moon.
The legshop keeper corrects me:
Those aren't wolf legs, those are
jackal legs, four dollars the pair.
Never mind, give me a pair of those green
dragon legs with scales,
today I feel I could settle
things with St. George, and maybe
get to keep the maiden.
Oh, those? the shop keeper says,
those are just old iguana legs,
dollar a leg, I give you two
for a buck fifty.
Way down at the end of the counter
a pair of legs in fishnet
sway their knees to music,
tapping their toes.
Those legs, I want those legs,
so the shop keeper pronounces us
husband and wife.

Now we have four legs.
We snort fire.
We howl at the moon:
owooo woooo owoooo.

David W. Jones—*trained in city planning and natural resources conservation, and one of the founders of Friends of the Chicago River—canoes that body of water frequently.*

"I am always fond of the statement, 'Every poem is a love poem.'"

ROBERT JONES

FRONT PORCH AT HOME

My mother sweeping off the porch at home
upon a twilight street remains in sight.
She is so busy, beautiful and white.
Filled fruit trees in the backyard grow in loam.
Cherries and pears are there and grapes that foam
into a purple pulp to cook at night
into preserves beneath a kitchen light.
She disappears somewhere, sheen hair to comb.

Time passes and my mother's not still young,
nor do the trees have fruit, eternal Fall.
A gradual hum of years at last has stung
mine with a shadowed fading, shrinking small.
When she has gone, my lamentations sung,
she'll be a memory near some ivied wall.

Robert Jones, *a longtime resident of Chicago's North Shore, can turn out a sonnet in seven minutes.*

"The end of all our exploring...beyond home or childhood is to go back and know where we are for the first time. To make an end is to make a beginning..." —T. S. Eliot

MARYANN GALVIN KOFOED

CICADAS IN MOTION

Cicadas with the Tiffany lamp wings
inch up the tree trunk, afraid they will break.

Punctual wayfarers, they come with instructions
only to propagate and sleep again.
My son, Paul, makes an amusement park for them,
a circular tract of leaves and twigs.
The cicadas jerk over the carpet of plenty,
tight-rope walk a stick on their way to green sun.

They've left the cramp of burial,
their fetal position,
and crackle time in slow motion.
Movement is what counts. Eight-year-olds know this.
They are certain if you had
one chance every seventeen years,
the thing you would most enjoy
in your time out
is to move.

Maryann Galvin Kofoed has an MA from Northwestern University and worked in publishing before raising four amazing children.

"Art without love is to open the wrong door." —Marc Chagall

PETER J. LAFORGE

ONCE

I snatched the ball off the boards,
fell to my toes, knees bent, pivoted
and took it down myself.

At the center line I was suddenly
aware of only me moving
into the next moment. I saw my own
slow dance, felt the bones move
in their sockets, watched the ball
float to and from my rubber hands
and God! I sang out loud: "Cruisin' down
the river on a Sunday afternoon" down
to the bottom of the key
where I woke to the roar,
saw Miller staring, passed to Scoop,
put my hands upon my knees and smiled
as though I'd just seen God.

Peter La Forge is a retired English teacher.

"Words and meaning, once they're allowed to go to bed together, allow the writer to surprise himself, make art possible, reveal how much of Being we haven't yet encountered." —Donald Bartholome

JOHN LINDBERG

GARDENING NAKED IN THE RAIN

you have to be careful
not to be seen
so it's best done at night
when the plants are asleep
and weeding and mulching
like prayers fulfill themselves
in trust for the morning
when the cabbage unrolls its leaves
releasing its image of you in the night
sunk to its green core
when you parted its green coils
to let in the soft rain.

MULBERRY LEAVES

fall after frost
simply let go
not even that watching I can't
see any start
simply they fall
still as the air
by scores
none at the same time
hundreds in air
spread like the squares
quilts build from scraps
golden the leaves
part from their twigs
easy as death
never a sigh
just their slight weight
drifts them away
the tree
naked as fate
stands above shreds
strewing the grass.

John Lindberg, a long-time college English teacher, writes poetry mostly to share with his students.

"Poetry is the spontaneous overflow of powerful feelings recollected in tranquillity." —William Wordsworth

ROBERT LINDNER

ANNE, AGE SIXTEEN

At the Silver River Resort
I stand on her cabin porch.
The Colorado River laughs, like her
Icy father at the door.

My sweater worn for good impressions
Has a hole in it.

I stand next to clock beats, as sun's
Golden sheaves wrap around twilight.
The Queen Anne's still in the mirror
With long looks, eyes getting painted
With the "danse macabre" mask
Of eroding grey lives.

She is a riddle: How can straight
Black hair make cross lines,
In a never intersecting parallel
A geometry of will and willow women,
When that waist-length hair swims,
With the wind names like Mariah
In your copy book?

KISS AT THE BLACK CANYON

Camera, its timer catches us
Arched like a natural bridge
Shadows under the protection of
The earth's oldest base rocks
In the "Black Canyon."

The Gunnison River cuts like
Sweet breath on the harmonica,
We lie on the steam. Oo-wee
I can't wait for fingers
On your rail steel guitar.

A mid-summer's puberty song
Of wet naked frogs barely
Outgrown their tadpole tails
We're Etched in the rock wall
Next to "JanetlovesPete '32,"
Carved in a heart shape.
Dragonfly wedding processions,
Hover on threads of sunlight,

Droning, "Yes sir, that's my
baby, no sir, don't mean maybe."

The mosquitoes chased us off
The males whining for sex.
The females biting for blood.

GRAND MESA LUPINE

We're here in the foreground,
Of the road up to the Grand Mesa,
One of the worlds widest
High plateaus, 10,000 feet high.
She is my girl of long lupine mesa,
The sunset on her red hot bluffs,
She is Paris in "The Fall,"
With street musicians, with artists
Drawing brows on my pulcinellas.

We're in Fruita, Utah
By the giant dinosaur statue
At the train station.
The eyes of the California Pacific,
Children, come to windows,
"Tyrannosaurus rex!" and laugh
At me, whistling Petrouchka,
My patchwork heart, bursting
Love with inconstant angles,
My oblong, awkward steps
Mimic spasms of heat.

In the horizon, I sing to her.
The moon is a maiden,
A ballad of comings and goings.
I find my voice rising.
The moon is my lover.
I battle storm cloud warriors
On the grand mesa to rescue her.
Kissed me a thousand years.

Missed me until spring, when
She came to the meeting place
Of the Gunnison and Colorado
Late at night, on a train,
The platform rumbling thunder.
I held roses with baby's breath,
She smiled the moon to rise.

BABOON ORGAN TRANSPLANT

Man has evolved. Once
conquering tribes lay waste to the field,
ate the hearts of their enemy,
ate the brains of their ancestors,
returned to the mazes of thorn bushes.

Man has evolved. Once
the skin of the male lion
wrapped
the god head of homo sapiens aboriginalis,
stone man, bronze man, iron man, his pride,
his sexual prowess, his large harem.

Man has evolved. Once
victorious horsemen cut the plains,
stealing women, striking male primate chests,
turning "old tortoise" on its back,
taking energy from its cruel degradation.

Man has evolved. Once
feathers of the eagle dressed the priest-doctor,
guardian of gardens, of truth trees, of intellect,
lifting the knife of belief, the cup of dominion,
belched smoke, beat drums, gargoyled nonbelievers.

Man has evolved. Now
dominant culture structures a tower of Babel,
looks at the world through eyes of the cannons,
turns human waste into fodder, burns gasoline,

tears open the abdomens of young baboons
cuts out their livers to save lives,
kills one primate, kills another,
takes the subhuman organs
calls them Baboons,
vicious apes, not evolved.

Robert Lindner, *born in a displaced persons' camp in Austria to Jewish parents from Poland, has a PhD in biochemistry and is a physician in public health involved with caring for center city and rural poor.*

"Writers...cannot reproduce reality unchanged...It is inevitable... that science should." —*Sigmund Freud*

BRUCE LOEWENTHAL

BIRD 2

An uneasy population
Pushes a massive nose
Into syrupy vegetation of television;
Charles Parker leaping across
Into this modern world.
Spirit in flight, Bird in poem,
Buddha in his alto fingers
Tipping traditions, bending branches
of harmonic ideas.
Fulfilling musical sparks,
Flowering fountains of air
On stages blowing, breathing fresh phrases,
Sweetening life on Earth.
The lark never missing a cadence,
Headwater of a roaring mountain stream,
Source of expanding dawns,
Shorelines of a new romantic age.

Bruce Loewenthal has a special fondness for jazz as well as for baseball.

"Poetry is a chronicle on the condition of man for all ages."

KATHLEEN B. MADDOX

THE LAKE

The lake was blue and pleasant in the sun;
The herons harvested the frogs along the shore,
Standing reed-like at the water's edge before
Their stately stroll resumed. Fat spiders spun
Their gauzy dinner plates, and beetles raised
Somehow above all beetle-kind, walked
On the water. The emerald grass-snake stalked
His smaller kin, and by his beauty praised
Whatever god made serpents beautiful.
The cricket chorus soft piped the dark.
And like old memories, up rose the moon.
Over the misty lake the air was full
Of the voice of eternal loneliness—the stark
Unanswered questioning of the loon.

Kathleen B. Maddox, after a stroke and now 87, still "dictates" in her writing group in Ypsilanti, Michigan.

"Let.../The swan on still St. Mary's Lake/Float double, swan and shadow." —*William Wordsworth*

CHRIS MANDELL

IN THE NURSING HOME

Fingers that had once fed children
now juggle like gnats,

feeding her old eyes
with wide shock.
Sheets drape her bones
as snow drapes comfort over rocks.
In a frozen huddle,
her limbs bend
for a final, subtle leap.

THE HOMELESS

Some take refuge in silence,
huddling fetally,
having no home but that one remembrance.

Some speak uncontainably,
having no walls to hold the words in.

Some rage at each other,
having no space to save rage for those
who are anyhow too sheltered
from their own hearts to care.

A NIGHT TOGETHER ON THE BEACH

roped boats chatter on the far dock
waves swerve from sand to sea
stars loosen in their sockets
and for a moment our names are lost

Chris Mandell is a violinist, artist, and teacher who lives in Boston.

"all ignorance toboggans into know and trudges up to ignorance again" —*e. e. cummings*

SHERRI LEDERMAN MANDELL

AFTER BIRTH

They splish on to the floor
shedding their dark sacs.
She licks them off
and growls
at pigeons,
will not leave
her shelf of space.

The puppies have not opened
their eyes. They could be little cows
or birds, pulsing hearts
still bound to the twin mothers
of sleep and breast,
the kingdom of soft grunts.

It takes time to adjust
to this world of light,
to see everything
in its corner.
Each rock seems about to burst
into a million different pieces.

Everything wants to be born again.

PEACOCKS

Others think they can water your feathers
and grow their own bouquet.
They don't know what a sadness it is

to carry yourself always like a king.
All these years you have paraded,
trailed by a host of luminescent eyes

but denial has claimed your deepest attention.
You cannot acknowledge the child
offering you her crusts.

Go ahead and shriek.

You were cursed with the need
to defend your reflection.

RIDING

"The will is given us that we may know the delights
of surrender."
   —Denise Levertov

You lead your horse down the steep bank
into cold water,
surveying rock shadows
to discover a path
that will not swallow you

But you cannot judge
the water's depth,
only its swiftness
so you lift your legs from the stirrups
to hug his neck as he transports you, knee-deep,
across a stream whose currents forbid trespass.

He leads you through poison oak
and wild gardenias, thickets and thick
grass. Your blood splashes,
dissolving bonds.
His legs become your own.
When he drinks, your reflection
glides downriver.

He leads you up to where
the earth reverses itself
opening into plateau
painted with lupine and sage,
a lap where you rest,
feel him breathing in your knees.

Mountains swallow your name.
Your voice discovers its sister.

Galloping,
you are quicker than the river.

Sherri Lederman Mandell *is the mother of three small children, has an M.A. in creative writing, and teaches technical writing at the University of Maryland.*

"What the poet is trying to accomplish is to discover relationships that give life: mental, physical, and imaginative life, the fullest and most electric sense of being." —James Dickey

ROBERT Mc CRAY

POETIC JUSTICE

When McCready was 17 he wrote "beginnings."
    Stars splashed against the sky, rockets zoomed,
    young girls walked into winter rain.
Young and bold, he hurled images
    like thunderbolts, rode bucking metaphors
    up anapestian stanzas, and
exploded in roaring galaxies of outer space.

The audience cheered, rose from bucket seats
to watch stars collide, rockets disappear
    and wipe the sting of winter rain from their faces,
and waited for endings—that never came.

When McCready was 37 he wrote "middles."
    burning coals cauterized the night, creative sparks
blistered
    almond-eyed woman lounged in dactylic doorways.
Seasoned and versed, he polished graven images
    like diamonds, handrubbed similes
    until they glistened, and
explored the antibacchian chores of inner space.

The audience nodded, leaned forward on cushioned seats
to study sparkling gems, internal milky ways of tetrameter
      wiped silver spondee dust from their eyes,
and waited for endings—that never came.

When McCready was 67 he wrote on;
      elysian groves beckoned, eagles soared,
        sylvan women leaped rununculus streams
Gnarled and wizened, he chopped iambics
      like icons, hiked pyrrhic peaks
        over haiku horizons, and
explored the darkening verse.

The audience wheezed, gloved aluminum
      walkers up worn aisles
        wiping dry tears from their cheeks,
and left before...the final ending.

Bob Mc Cray *teaches journalism in a community college.*

"You will find poetry nowhere unless you bring some with you."
—Joseph Joubert

COLLEEN Mc MANUS

GONE

the ghost of him
shims through her
as he passes
she is standing at the kitchen sink
her fingers lost
in a slur of soap
and he flickers a memory
wavering, his old self
holding her—
mouth against her hair
she drops her head, staring
into the drain

the sensation slipping past now
harder to save
than the stream of water
against her wrist

and he comes at night
when she is gone, safe
behind her eyes, closed
to the seeping light
of the street
she is beyond
her body that barely lifts
the sheet with the
rise and fall of her breasts
he is a dream
but so warm, his skin
she can feel the bones beneath
and he is opening his mouth
his voice in her ear, clear
but the words splinter
and drift, fading
even as she reaches
to gather them
jagged puzzle pieces of his mouth
his shirt pocket
his hand around a glass

and even these
melt when she opens her eyes
only knowing
he was there by the press
of the empty space
against the inside
of her

Colleen McManus *works, goes to college, takes care of her young twins.*

"The act of writing requires a constant plunging back into the shadow of the past where time hovers ghostlike." —*Ralph Ellison*

KAT MEADS

RECKONING

Whether or not you wish to hear it I tell
the story now. It happened in Florence. He
was not a big man though he imagined himself to be.
I had a fever, forgot to lock the door. When he fell
upon me I could not reach the bell
or his throat, my hands pinned between
his chest and mine. I remember
his smell,
the staggered syllables I could not understand.
As in the movies it happened. Not here
in our land of mutual consent: a woman
and man at home with love and lust, volunteering
a tangle of sheets. Here or in
Florence—beneath ceilings, men.

Kat Meads, born and raised in the South, currently lives in California.

"Rhyme...adds a sound effect, a clang in your mind."
—Anne Sexton

HARRIET J. MELROSE

IT ONLY HAPPENED ONCE

My father brought me a present,
once, from a principals' forum,
paper dolls and costume cut-outs.

I threw a fork at him
when I was five. It landed
in his cup, spattered his
best suit and brand new tie.

He put me across his knee
that one time and spanked me.

I stood proudly when he
won the Alumni Medal.
With Mr. Citizen, the Y award,
each new plaque screamed,
he was a father
to everyone but me.

When Martin Luther King
died, high school kids gathered
at our house. My father's
was the only ghetto school in
Connecticut that escaped the riots.

I never let him hug me.
I'd cringe as though his skin
were poison when my lips brushed
his forehead out of obligation.

He asked me to forgive him
one month before he died.
His ticker was getting old,
he said, we were running
out of time.

For one moment, our
booth by the bar in Finnegan's
seemed transported to the moon.
I felt stranded—
every voice disappeared.

I can still feel my parched
throat unable to say
the words he wanted to hear.

Harriet J. Melrose' *work was aired on "Dial-A-Poem, Chicago!" several times and included in <u>The Real Dragon Project</u>, a collection of poetry distributed to political prisoners.*

"...poetry exists to break through to below the level of reason where angels and monsters that amenities keep in the cellar may come out to dance, to rove and roar, growling and singing...." —May Sarton

JESSE MILLNER

MY BACK ROADS

A dark highway runs east of the Blue Ridge,
passes occasional towns that sleep
and squander the moonlight.
Charlottesville and my life, lie dimly ahead
but now bare-topped mountains sing
from rattlesnake heights,
cool sky tumbles down,
rushes through low windows,
wakens my skin.

A cooler waits in the back seat,
my right arm reaches
grabs a glistening bottleneck.
Frayed silver eyes of stars peek
through breaks in black-boned night,
warm air escapes
from woods and fields,
smells like damp hollows,
is filled with shrill crickets.

My right foot pushes harder,
narrows this asphalt ribbon,
miles gain, empty bottles
rattle to the beat of potholes,
as my heart quickens,
an engine run hard.

For a moment, I'm five-years old again,
racing with my father

down the Crewe to Burkville road
in his old, grey Ford.
He wears Old Spice and sweat, smokes
fast Camels as the high
summer and Virginia wildness
rush up to the heat-stained blacktop.
We pass miles of pine, yellowgreen tobacco,
honeysuckle on rusted barbed wire;
I taste a fragrance of tired fields
and wilderness
as my father reaches under the front seat,
pulls out a brown bag, drinks deeply,
and smiles, his face turning red.

OUTDOOR CAFE DISTANCES

In coffeehouse shadows,
moonlight collects on faces
of silverware,
reflects off your earrings,
brightens the ragged skies
of my half-open windows.
Your eyes are miles of mountain starlight
filled with invitation
to leave this grey-stained city
I have become.

Cups rattle, strangers whisper
as I listen in sin,
and graze on the damp fur of rumor.
But then your voice sighs
through my hollows

and I push away from those shallows of myself,
force my fingers across distances
to find hands that beckon
toward
your sweet and foreign country.

BOTTOMLAND SONG

In praise of hunting,
my grandfather
walks through the high chestnut trees,
and old twelve-gauge
held tight
in his brown weathered hand.
Autumn leans in cool,
and beyond the yellow leaves
a pale sun climbs
the seamless morning sky.

Eight years old,
I follow him down
a brown carpeted hill,
our steps bring crisp sighs
to the calm woods
as we descend to
bottomland.

Where a creek cuts through red clay,
muddy brown water
rushes past moss-covered stones,
and tadpoles race the shallows;

I cup my hands in cold water
catch nothing,
but feel everything
in the steady pulse of current.

WHAT FRIGHTENS ME

I am troubled by people
breaking into
the cluttered basement
of my life.
They look too closely at dusty frames;
my ex-wife young,
that picture luminous with hope,

crimson with desire;
it burns and darkens before their eyes.

Then the well hidden self-portrait,
whiskey-stained, vacant skyed,
at a strange angle
to its surroundings
because the man has wings
that beat and bleed slowly,

as I rustle like a large dark bird
and frighten them,
these intruders
who have never heard
a painting speak.

Jesse Millner, who is teaching and working on his MFA at Florida International, was born in rural Virginia, grew up in cities out west; so the landscapes he dreams are tangled and strange and always have a southern accent.

"...the poem was born elsewhere...like the wild geese of the Arctic it heads home, far above the borders, where most things cannot cross."
—Gary Snyder

ROBERT MILLS

A GAGGLE OF POEMS ALMOST IN FLIGHT

Thrust from the nest
these sparrows are on their own.

Hen-sparrow did what it had to;
the progeny must become themselves

for the hen resumes its life,
hostile to the offspring

yet cannot help but wonder
will they be graceful in the air?

Even expand it ever so slightly
like a flower unfolding the light?

And what's it like
to thrill to the size of the sky?

UNANSWERED DIALOGUE

High summer all the way up to the sun,
clouds are swelling armadas.
They roam the wind
       in an ungoverned sky.

On the ground
we are Cain's children
voiceless and solemn
God and man in wordless dialogue

considering the dark center of solitude
overwhelmed
by weight of bitterness
yet wading through the quiet

listening always
for first sounds of a pair of swallows
burning bright and quick
       high overhead.

Robert Mills, *former administrator, is now spending his life learning to write poetry.*

"Poetry may be defined as a way of remembering what it would impoverish us to forget." —Robert Frost

EDWARD MORIN

SYLVIA SKIING

Snow breeze powders your cheek:
the sun shines like cold fur.
Jacket sleeves squeak at your sides
and your knees bend against tough jeans.
Gravity is a current pulling.

The beginning is almost tedious—
picking the mark for a first turn.
Traffic is light. You have to sway
like a pine against
going too fast
before the first mogul.

What large feet to find their way
easily without stubbing.
Flying all courage past a birch,
you laugh away the scare
of being a casualty.

Banking hunchback at each mogul—
third, fourth, fifth—gets more
urgent and slipshod, yet anyone
but you would call it graceful.
Halfway down. You bite bigger
sliced curves that won't bend enough.

At last you're worried
water running downhill.
Bottom rushing closer,
you lift off a straight jump—
wind crackling in your ears—
and sail the length of two breaths

until a white dust cloud
explodes, catches, glides
you back onto the cold
bright, slowing earth.

Edward Morin has had poems published in Hudson Review, Ploughshares, and his book The Dust of Our City; songs on the cassette Transportation: Hot Tunes and Blues from Motor City; and translations in TriQuarterly, Iowa Review, and his anthology The Red Azalea: Chinese Poetry Since the Cultural Revolution.

"We must pass through solitude and difficulty, isolation, and silence, in order to reach forth to the enchanted place where we can dance our clumsy dance and sing our sorrowful song...the most ancient rites of our conscience in the awareness of being human and of believing in a common destiny." —*Pablo Neruda*

LOUELLEN MURRAY

MUTATIONS

>>>>Some things
>>>folks are just born knowing,
>>like how to sweet talk trouble
>>away, never to lock doors, to party
>>>down, and there is
>>no such thing as the last
>>>>fire
>>>of the season.

>Other things folks hear beyond
>>>>remembering:
>>>the whereabouts of our great-
>great-grandparents during the War,
>>>the essence of an
>>apple, that it takes three
>>>>logs, but only one
>>>>>match
>>>to kindle a blaze.

>>>>Folks
>>>stray far from home,
>like kites with tails in tatters,

sailing in foreign wind,
our ancestral fabric like inherited
quirk. The casualties of geography,
we question our sacred idiosyncrasies,
prefer not our home-spun
genius for making
do.

What if folks cut adrift, forget
manners, permit the cup that is less than
silver to graze our
lips, and stock our outcast
selves with materials so
raw, that never gave
comfort
to anyone before.

Still we spawn
new folks inside whose
bones know and remember, navigate
past parent
excesses
and collect their family
inheritance.

Louellen Wright Murray, *a graduate in geography from Georgia State, gardens and golfs, teaches and writes, while balancing three children, a black cat, and an investment banker husband.*

"This is not it at all/That is not what I meant at all." —T. S. Eliot

ALLISON J. NICHOL

CANCER SCARE

I called you because your mother called me.
The lump is small, imperceptibly so. It can't be
felt or seen or heard, or so the doctor said. How
can something with no form have such power to start

my heart to racing, curl into a child
frightened by too many losses to the failed

miracles of medicine. Calling you
my fingers dialed all the right numbers,
like walking home in the dark. Your voice was cool
to the touch. My own, fragile as a book teetering
on a top shelf, that could be set to sail by
the first strong breath.

Two years is a long time between sentences.
Our conversation swirled around itself, pale
and thin as smoke in a jar. I asked how you were,
meaning I missed you. I said I knew in my heart
your mother would be fine, meaning the thought
of losing her was too scary to even give birth
to whisper. You asked your second favorite question.
I answered yes, but I'm down to less than half
a pack a day. We both agreed we hated exactly
the same person, for completely different reasons.
I said good-bye, meaning, measure for measure, you
are still one of the best people I have ever known.

SAN ANTONIO STROLL

We found ourselves by accident,
following the stone path that wound
like a rumor just below the city's
surface. Suddenly we were surrounded
by bluebonnets and bougainvillea
bathing naked in the first sprinkle
of spring sunlight. Blackbirds nuzzled

their young in the shade of a shaggy
elm. Water, stolen from god, ambled
at our feet slow as a late August breeze.
Startled by this beauty,
you clenched my arm.
I stumbled a smile
that fell forward to your lips, certain
all creation was inviting us to kiss.

ORIGINAL SIN

My best friend Teresa said I had
the most original sins of anybody
in the whole fifth grade.
As we huddled in the back pew,
co-conspirators, lace doilies dangling
precariously from bobby pins stuck
in our heads like thumbtacks. Our hands
folded in semi-automatic position, fingering
the familiar circle of glass beds
slowly enough to avoid scrutiny. Sweat
tickling our backs under summer wool
uniforms as we waited our turns, giggling
like spies, concocting great tales
of broken commandments. Sins, venial
and mortal turning over on our tongues,
coating our teeth like sugar.

Allison J. Nichol is publisher of the <u>Queer Planet Review</u> and Chicago's Dial-A-Poem.

"If fiction is a lie about the truth, then poetry is the truth about the truth."

B. Z. NIDITCH

DEATH SQUADS

Remember:
The First,
when grey birds
were speechless
and torture
smothered our whispers.

Remember:
The Second,
when the dirt
condemned our mouth
from speaking
out of blood.

Remember:
The Third
a love letter
was banned
but the guards watched
enraged at the morning.

Remember:
The Fourth,
newspapers full of fish
were cited
no mirrors spoke rumors
no skin is pale
as milk.

Remember:
The Fifth,
he never made it
to the door,
skulls are silent
on graffiti walls
and his heart stopped.

Remember:
The Sixth,
the wind was here,
life demands coffee
and bluebirds
and love letters
and blood.

B. D. Niditch *is the artistic director of the Original Theatre.*

"Poetry is translation into our own heaven."

MOIRA NOLAN

LIFE STARTS AT FIFTY

For the bitter bread we now eat alone
the sweat of our palms paid cash,
while jingling pennies and coupons
humbly silence their rustle
unlike the rusting leaves that fall
on the November of our lives.

We lay the lawnmower to rest
in the lean-to, summer flashed.
Under its sun spots we forgot for a time
the cold of our single pillowed beds;
we crawl now in old socks and slippers,
frayed robes; only the spider we spared
in the backroom window corner knows us.
A late night TV host on his side
of his glass prison cannot shame the folds
of our neck and jowls, the dust we let set,
grey snow, on the bibelots of our life.

Some of us buy into pretend youth,
join health clubs, patronize single bars,
but land on arthritic feet, at two a.m.,
still alone and still old inside,
under spandex and silicon.

Summer needed its edges trimmed. Late Autumn
empty afternoons we trudge our way to Kroger.
All-Saints day crowds offer us nothing but shoves,
mug us for pennies, for grocery coupons.
Under our arm the last spidery mum on sale,
precious find, we walk around the mall, all faces
those of strangers and we hurry, worrying,
last soul of post, that we have forgotten
to turn over the calendar page at home.

Moira Nolan has lived throughout Europe and the United States, and now makes her home in Kentukyana and teaches in a junior college.

"I am the mature woman, self-willed, on the seventh path to wisdom."

ALICE OLDS-ELLINGSON

CHILDHOOD

When the train whistles
like a bad song at me,
It is telling me I'm alone.
Mommy's gone on the train
gone with Daddy far away
on a moon. I say it out loud
in the dark.

No, I don't.
I have a train whistle here
in my blue bed that's blue
under a blue blanket I tuck me in.
I have a midnite and a four
in the morning. AND I DON'T
HAVE A TUMMY ACHE. I don't.

Lloyd runs away from me.
Lloyd doesn't like me.
They left me with him.
He's too little to call the doctor.
I'll ask Joy to take him away
and spank the daddy out of him.
Joy is fat. She's NOT my Mommy.

She lies. She tells me
my mommy is coming back.

She looks at me that funny, sad way.
She's another train whistle.
I don't believe her at all.
Coming back SOON.
They went away on the train that
whistles.
They left me like a blue blanket.
That's me in the picture with a frog.

AFTER THE DOCTOR TELLS ME I'M DYING

Clouds don't have ulterior
designs on me today.
They don't look guilty
like animal faces or the visages
of Satan. Satan is out of
the question. (God never did
exist.)

From my indoor point of view
the envelopes of moisture
look cold. I am drinking
ice water. Maybe I shall get a cup
of coffee and warm the picture up.
But, not just yet.

I like sitting here across the room from Mom sharing the skies
with her. Not saying anything
about the slant
of winter sun.

This still, white calm will last.
Tomorrow,
I can go somewhere. Or the day after.
I am not going to die.

Alice Olds-Ellingson, before tragedy (and paralysis) struck, was an English teacher and secretary.

"'He who laughs last didn't get the joke' I like dry or wet humor—everywhere."

JOAN POLIKOFF

TO NADIA COMANECI

Nadia, to reporters enquiring about your married lover
who abandoned his wife in seething Romania,
to engineer your escape,
you replied, "So?"
your eyebrow attaining an unparalleled arch.

In Maxim's you spoke rudely to the waiter
and the people at the next table cringed.

We ache
for the precision
of your small toes.
We yearn
for the purity
of your flight,
asking

give us
grace.

BEFORE YOU LEAVE

Your hands holding mine feel cold;
bruises bloom violets
beneath your thumbs.
Your voice jangles, distant—
I hear a gathering cry in my chest.
Seeking my accustomed rest
in the balance of your features,
I am caught
in the mask
of your face.

Fleeing,
my skeleton rocks
moored in channels of blood.

My heartbeat
calls me home.

Is it only skin that holds me—
Weaves threadtight my fear,
ligament,
and breath?
Keeps me from coming apart
like leaves falling?

What trunk or stalk
will be left?

Perhaps my bones
a small, shining heap
no blood
anywhere.

MY COUSIN'S LOVER DIES FROM AIDS

The bishops bob like lilies at the altar
above the body
quite catholic.

Spanked by a rap tune playing on the street,
the cathedral walls shroud the family,
remote as street lamps.

Outside, children moondance.
Mourners inside stumble to their feet,
trying to recall the holiness of last communion
when they swallowed God
in bite-size pieces.

My cousin's palm sweats inside mine.
Above, Christ is loosed
from the life-size crucifix suspended
above the coffin.

Joan Polikoff, a psychotherapist in a community health center, seeks Wisconsin open spaces, Colorado mountain peaks, and quiet.

"Stay fluid behind those black-and-white words. They are not you. They were a great moment going through you."
—Natalie Goldberg

HELEN G. REED

HER HUSBAND'S DEATHS
(For H.K.G. and H.F.G.)

The first time my father died
my mother fluttered,
sensed a dark presence—
a great cat, haunched to pounce.
Her half-blind eyes mapped
the shadow-hill and valleys
of his face this one more time,
her fingers ran the falter
of pulse in his neck.
He folded his hands across his chest—
this great gasping salmon, worn out
by the long punishing upstream drive—
released his breath into the room.

She felt the grey cat rise.

She hovered close,
eyes fear-enameled white.
Then, even as he slipped quietly
toward long-awaited sleep,
she quickly leaned and snagged him—
as she'd seen him hook a strong finger
through a fish's gasping gills—
pulled him back to her with the taut
singing line of her need.

As so many times before,
he woke to her.
His jaws seized air.
He chewed and swallowed it,
that sacrament to life.

The second time my father died,
years later, she was too weak
to hook his dulled coppery struggles,
to pull him back again.

LIKE LOVE
(For E.B.F.)

Poetry opens life up,
sweeps the dusty corners,
brings the scrapbook
up to date;
calls birds
back into trees,
prunes ragged shrubs,
readies the soil
for sprouting seeds
we never knew
could grow.

WOMEN'S BODIES

We are the dark rivers
on which they launch
their midnight explorations,
those deep stunned wanderings
unsatisfied
in tame easy waters
meandering nearby fields.

They plunge in frothing rush
toward branches,
deep-cut narrow beds,
currents misdirected.

Thunder toward undertows and riptides,
the sweet wind-songs of sirens,
the creaking songs of whales.

While we eddy—
flickering soft sandy lights—
in the shallows near home,
they wait for roiling clouds,
tumults of wind, shipwrecks
to deliver
from dream-wanderings
back to warm bed—
familiar hand on thigh;
tumbling, gently sheet-bound,
breath-to-breath
again.

DARING

She arrived, crashed into my pre-teen dreaminess,
pulled me out of childhood.
Her eyes flared white with energy
held in check—except for the dark electric shiver
of her hair. Doll houses, books forgotten,
I swept along in her surge. We climbed trees;
skated backwards; balanced our way across
the railroad trestle, above the river.
We rode vines
out over the swift water.

Summer nights we darted—silvery fish—
through leaf-seined green beneath streetlights,
standing up, no hands, bicycles steadied
between our knees. Whatever was there
to be dared, she'd do.
With me just behind.

But she—a year older—suddenly went from scissoring-
out magazine pictures of our favorite movie stars
to looking like one. From tomboy to cover girl
overnight. Boys—straining to catch a glimpse—their eyes

slicing the stretch of fabric across the deepening V
of her chest, the rounding thighs; they, hurled into silence
by a slow-motion toss of her newly-timed hair.

Lost in their sniggering whispers,
I watched her swagger disappear
into inviting small movements, moods
musky and fogged. There, for once,
I could not—
dared not yet—follow.

Helen Reed *enjoys words and birds and, like "Mary, Mary," watches her garden—of opalescent pitchers—grow.*

"...how deep were the complexities of the everyday, of the family, what caves were in the mountains, what blocked chambers, and what crystal rivers that had not yet seen light." —Eudora Welty

ANTHONY RIPLEY

AUTUMN LOVE SONG

He paused raking suburban leaves
into heaps the wind blew away.
Beer might be an answer,
or at least an alibi,
to go inside.

A sound stopped him—
Unseen geese, wild and high above,
flying maybe 50 miles an hour in flapping vees,
repeating old family arguments
on the pecking order
or where to stop that night.

The sound babbled down, faint and mysterious.
Stirring old harmonies, old dissonances.
"Mated for life," he said out loud. "It's magic."

"What's tragic?" asked his gloomy neighbor
who never listened well,
and always looked for other walking wounded
to limp with him awhile.

"It's tragic standing here without a beer,"
the raker said, and turned to go,
giving up on leaves falling, flying,
chasing him, a plague of monarch butterflies.

He tiptoed to the living room.
She dozed over murders on her lap.
Close to her side, he whispered
through cold beery lips
the words they both had chosen
to pledge their freestyle troth
in bell-bottomed trousers, print dresses,
in a farmer's field with scattered corn to feed the geese:

> I have one life to lead. You have become central
> to that life. We are bonded, you and I,
> for all our days. We are wild geese.

Her eyes still closed, she began the argument.
"You mean to say you woke me up
just to tell me that?"
Then couldn't fake it any more,
and tickled him instead.

CONFESSIONS OF A PALLBEARER

The wooden box was cheap, and light enough—
white pine upholstered in brown moleskin
for he was now to dwell among the moles.

We pallbearers were but
a clutch of cranky newsmen
all reaching out for history
(which lies
hidden within truth
and is a fool for speculation.)

Fort Worth, Texas, on an average afternoon,
the cemetery grass November yellow,
reporters pushing for handholds
along the coffin,
undertaker flunkies in black suits,
county sheriff's deputies uncomfortable
in the otherwise deserted burial ground
as crowds of several hundred gaped outside,
held back by chain-link fencing.

We crowded round the dyecast handles
or just reached out to touch the shabby box,
doing bizarre honor to the corpse,
Lee Harvey Oswald.
He wore the standard uniform
issued for cheap funerals.
His suit and shirt were dickeys with no backs.
That's what the undertaker told us.

And though we carried Oswald,
we weren't allowed to look inside.
The box was only opened
when his wife and relatives arrived
in Secret Service cars, another irony,
coming down the dusty road
to where we'd put the box on straps
to let it down six feet.

Thirty years ago I never thought to ask
the fundamental question:
Why did he do it?
We were driven almost wild just covering
the other basics.

MOTHS

A small gray moth,
romanced by the television light
and slow enough for capture by Nathaniel,

flew between the La-Z-Boy chair
and the glowing picture tube
in the darkened family room
where scarcely any family
ever spread its wings these days.

Tired from a day of reproduction,
the moth was searching comfort—
a woolen bassinet
for the last of her eggs.
She tarried too long,
drunk and disorderly
in the room's only light.

Nate, lurking in the shadows,
saw his chance and lunged,
clapped his hands prayer-like on the moth
then slowly opened them,
searching palms and fingers
for the gray smear of success.
There was none.
Perhaps his reflexes had slipped another notch.

He did not curse the moth for cleverness.
Besides, no one was home to hear his curses spilling out,
and Nate husbanded his truly pungent language
for the evening television news,
which he hated worse than moths.
His roaring then was loud enough
to stir a million hungry larvae
and rouse his wife, Gladys, from the kitchen phone
to which she surgically attached herself in evenings
after a day as a hospice volunteer.

When the hollering began
Gladys always worried
what the neighbors might think—
that they were fighting or making love.
"Nate, will you never stop the shouting?"
she always shrieked, outraged.

And he would always roar his answer:
"Happy Bottom, you old whore,
shut your fried and flappy lips."

Nate, the killer, found a moth
more challenging than Gladys for the moment.
He lurched himself to sitting upright in the chair,
rose on cranky ankles and splayed feet
and went for bugspray in the back hall closet.
Back on the recliner once again,
he lay in ambush.

The moth, frustrated by imitation wool carpeting,
tasteless cotton drapes,
and rubber-filled fake leather cushions,
tried another intoxicating run
past the candle colors of TV.

Nate flattened her with poison gas,
then dozed through Wheel of Fortune.
He dreamed of making love with Vanna White,
an old man with spent seed
in awkward moves with a television star.
When he awoke he found the moth's small corpse
on his woolen cardigan and picked her up.

Her tiny abdomen still writing;
a reflex after death,
she planted one last egg upon his hand
in nature's never ending search
for immortality.

THE BUREAUCRAT WORKS LATE

Now that the lights in the other offices are off,
Now that the cleaning man has come and gone—

        stamping, surly to my office
        to gut my bulging basket,
        hurling back the empty shell.

Now that the hardness of the day's demeaning arguments is
done, laved over by the silence of the building in the evening,
I sit among my papers. They will not hurt me.

I am a player in a game of rubber rules.
I am their bulldog manager
with rubber teeth, and rubber stamp
and rubber brain and rubber heart.

I will endlessly spring back from this day's loss.
I will gather strength from memos,
grace from interoffice mail.
The power from ignoring ringing phones
will flood my being,
with the radiance of a Presidential edict
declaring national rhubarb day.

I resume on Tuesday the trial by argument I lost today,
beginning with a clever killing memo on the hired help,
particularly emptiers of wastebaskets—they, surly crowd
that Tuesday night will carry off this memo,
the latest in my string of angry gestures
that stretches back to letters written
to John Foster Dulles in 1956,
protesting foreign policy
of nuclear retaliation
and of course,
never sent.
I mean,
what's the
p
o
i
n
t
?

Anthony Ripley, Harvard graduate and longtime writer-editor, lives in Colorado with his novelist-wife Ann.

"(The writer) must teach himself that the basest of all things is to be afraid; and, teaching himself that, forget it forever, leaving no room in his workshop for anything but the old verities and truths of the heart, the old universal truths lacking which any story is ephemeral and doomed—love and honor and pity and pride and compassion and sacrifice." —William Faulkner

RUTH ROMANENGHI

I CRY AT COMEDIES

I cry at weddings and circuses
and when buildings are razed.

I cry at the lake
when the sun is high
and people laugh
as they bask in it.

When a Basque basks, does he?

Once, I had a Basque dress,
having to do with seams and tucks.
I basked in it for its fitting bodice.
A bodice is modest.

I laughed a lot in that dress.
If I had a Basque dress now,
I might cry a little—
but never a lot.

My tears come
Smiling through a fudge sundae
in Sam's Ice Cream Emporium.
Despite the sweet dalliance,
my eyes shower, naked, in public.

Once, I cried at a beach party.
Somebody told me to jump in the lake.
Nobody knew I cried—
unless—the boy who rescued me?
He kissed my cheek.
Tears are salty.
I didn't marry him.

I married the boy I went to a wake with.
"For crying out loud," he said later,
"You just don't laugh at a wake."

I didn't tell him what I laughed at
nor remind him I was mostly Irish.

Ruth Romanenghi grew up in the Lincoln Park area—a "village" revisited in her poems and stories—and is working on a collection of Christmas tales.

Ralph Waldo Emerson sees poetry as "that region where the air is music."

MARYANN BENNETT ROSBERG

MAY 1: BELTANE

The rains have come
the snow's cold is over.
Thunder is heard again in the high places.
A great horned owl
was seen in a fir tree in a backyard.

Ad in the slit between water and sky
light passions to mauve
and all those embarrassing colors of desire.
The long branches breathe down into the water
and their reflection
reaches up, prolonging the longing.

It is the story of losing and finding
in the rising of the riverskin,
where you discover that everything feels like you
and nothing, no one is, and you want it all again.

Through a layered lace of leaves,
byzantine bees promise a sweet sting, if you come.
The pecking bird of blood red
drums fire into the joins of trees,
felt druid deep in the undersidal
blur of the mushroom decapped.
You rise wet from a lilac haze,
and slip on green dreams of grass
staining your clothes,
—rubbing the marks in, not out.

BACK TO THUNDERLINGS

Circling back to him on a leaden day,
to the other side of the moon, familiar, but not,
I cycle along the river road
that lows from one heartland to another.
Behind glass and steel,
I forget the old sounds,
but when I cycle, I listen to the crow pulse.
Trees clack until I look
and then they stand all stiffened spider hair,
veins for a summer fly's wing
—moving me even when they are still.
Coming late to his house,
I follow the polished stairs,
railings dark as rims for blue grey eyes
whitely balustered as his smile,
cool as a room swept free
of identifying dust by large hands
sure of brass knobs and keys:
an old lover's country, but only in my mind.

'Remember' rises with each step that leads me to him.
'Now?' falls with each shake of his hand in mine.

But the kiss I want to give stays with me.
In passing, I touch his black wool coat hung with rain,
I imagine from waiting for me, is still warm about the neck
with its underflow of silk.

There were all those days of wordmaking,
student and teacher,
hints in his voice, his skin like an open book,
nights speaking of dreams deep in the bone.
They must be, are here, still, after twenty years—in me.
Others always circled us with rings
I wear one, now; he had one, then.
More lines are in our faces than stretch between us.
More questions rise in me than fall from him.

We trace for each other, old turns, new bends.
Never asking, 'Did you, then?'
'Will you, now?' Never crossing our rings.

I return on a leaden night,
to my own country, cycling,
the familiar side of the moon above,
—his still unknown country in my mind.
Between us, the trees will grow another ring.

CAT ANNIE

Dying on her birthday,
Aunt Annie, Cat Annie, stalks at my side;
she's clinging to life so hard, she must have every bite.
Not knowing she's dead, yet, she leaves prints of the five wounds
in every step—

I want to talk with you about her, but you are too far away,
not as far as she, but now you both are imagery.

Falling snow makes dry little sounds like bone chips falling
on the ground, on my hood
and on the trees
who speak in the wind.

Sometimes clucking, squealing, creaking—
if trees were the first,
they taught the others to talk
—us last of all.
Then why can't I remember
the language?

Under the blood bird, the cardinal's song,
three geese fly low
over the bridge from here to there.
There's snow in every corner, but I know I've seen green tips
toppling the tense groundline...breaking the code.

I once felt a summer day
melt into summer night
—all movement ceasing. In the shadow of the skunk,
white stripe of lightning in the stillness.

We are such a combination of memory and body
—you climb into my eyes
and I remember child and lover.
Cat Annie climbs into my mind
and I hear the snow crow calling
the devouring mother:

Someone has to remember her;
she lives in us all.

I seemed to have stood on the edge of summer's leaf the last time
I talked with you.
The leaf is already laced and brown along the veins.
How long do we have?
until next spring, summer?
I thought we had forever.
Take another bite.

IN THE LAPWING OF THOUGHT

The leaves tacked
to my cork board
sing.

What we call voice
is rustles,
creaks.

When the soft life has
long gone from my leaves,
something is left
we could clone
and it would live on
a thousand fold the same.

Yet, if it went the way
it usually does,
a leaf would relife
in worms, in its own mother tree,
in honey bees, and me.

For leaves,
inner spiraled ladders
remember veined ways and sweet making
and perhaps the way sun licked a back.

Is that how I know leaving?

SNOW, GOING HOME

Snow comes just when I know
I can keep it away by wishing.
Then my car door will not close,
after I've pried it open.
I slam it again and again,
until, ice-boxlike
it clicks
and seals me in.

And I drive,
my headlights
holing a no-time tunnel
where I see a mammoth
of the future,
swinging tusks of light,

spraying saltrocks
to ease my way.

My car and I become
a surfaced submarine and
captain. Swashbuckling along,
I listen to the snow angel
siren singing
"close your eyes and let go"
into the white waters
to the seabed below.

A sudden slip
makes me grip the wheel.
In sailorsongs,
there waits one
who ports you
more than pole-stars
or trade winds,
who shores your
engulfing streams
—and I go home
to that one,
once more.

MaryAnn Bennett Rosberg's earliest memory of being a poet was in first grade, when she tried to convince her teacher that her poem about a forgotten cemetery was not really about the poor souls in purgatory.

"I want to know only that things gather themselves with great patience, that they do this forever." —Jared Carter

JOAN Z. ROUGH

AUGUST OBSERVED

Heated voices
Flare

The steel sky
Won't rain

Cool air
Curdles

Shrouds
Dusky landscapes

Geese land
Wired overhead

Wings fanning
Confetti stars

Suspended
On the rim

I stretch
Beyond the mist

Afternoon haze
The sun slips

Whispers vows
To yawing trees

Cornered shadows
Deepen
August hums
Swollen

Like the silver moon
The Buddha smiles

Joan Z. Rough *is an artist working in fine art photography and a volunteer naturalist/interpreter in Albemarle County, Virginia.*

"Poets are people who have momentarily stilled or silenced what-they-want-to say, so that they can speak." —Robert Kelly

CHARLOTTE ROYAL

TRAIN TO TOULON

On the table at dinner
a peach silk shaded lamp
shines the glass and silver

Shivers of motion tremble the wine
We drink Bordeaux and talk about our day

My flight was late
his anxious wait
my nervous searching for his face
and then the race to Gare de Lyon
still more delay
and we are gone

I touch his hand
holding a knife
slanted in air
and feel his eyes
warm on me
but when I dare
to raise mine
we cannot speak
I turn from light
and in the darkness see
retreating birches like
thin and dusky brides
left lonely in the night

He says my name
our crumpled napkins fall
we move along the corridor
in rocking single file
down our only aisle
to the dark compartment where
in the shadow
lies our narrow bed

calm now and ale
a shroud of cool white linen
with pillows head to head

Quick lighted windows
a silent rush of towns
silhouetted steeples
and flicks of sudden stars
the window shades stay up till dawn
speeding south to Toulon
and the sea

ANASTACIA

My mother's patience,   like a stone
never wore down,
lay   still as a pebble
in the white bed
washed in our words.
I said   once too often,
"You haven't been eating, Mother;
that's all it is...."

Her firm voice told me,
"Don't say that again. It's not true."
and then, "How long does it take to die?"
"Not long, Mother, not long," I hurried to say.

"It seems long," she said   and closed her eyes.
No right words came to me
eager to fluff her pillows   brush her hair
as she lay quiet   patient
a small rock of will   waiting for her
resurrection when the stone was rolled back
and light opened her eyes.

Charlotte Royal, *whom seven young men and women call Mother, is a travel agent who writes and paints when she in not up in the air.*

"Poetry must be hard and clear, never blurred or indefinite. It should not deal in generalities however magnificent and sonorous. Concentration is the very essence of poetry."

SARAH RUHL

THE EVOLUTION OF THE KISS

The embryonic moon-dipped
kiss of youth, two
fawns petting each
other flowers,
becomes eventually
(over squabbles, surprises, compromises
little deaths and little births
old and new appliances, compliance's)
The Middle Aged Kiss
enclosed in the dank
monasteries of the
Middle Ages
a squeezed-up
kiss wrung dry of
resentments and
overbred sentiment
that says with quiet
assent, yes dear, we
are for each other,
what else is there
to do, after all—I'm tired.

But now my parents
squeeze hands
under piles of
blankets every
night before
they let
sleep
anesthetize their
urge to sleep, pee,
and eat.

This squeeze is no
casual parting
for the night
but a triumph
over unscrewed-in lightbulbs,
over unwanted olives in the salad
and over unshared glances across
the kitchen table
a triumph over the
mornings of middle aged
kisses and a recognition
of the perils of sleep and love
made ritual
like the sign of the cross
or saying the same words
every time before you
hit the baseball or like
kneeling down in a white
robe under an Arab sun.

THE EVOLUTION OF A PHRASE CLOSE TO DYING

She used to write poems
that went clink-pretty
down the tall lemonade glass.
She used to write poems
that went pond-softy
into waiting heather.

Now she writes poems
that no one can hear;

The choke of the dying
is too loud.

Someone is retching in the
bathroom. She will write
phrases tied together with
mucus and vomit.

She will write them for
her father.

THE GLAD ANIMAL MOVEMENTS ALL GONE BY

I dream
my dead grandfather
I have never seen
coughing in a sick bed
next to my father

I walk around the house
dark with rich wood
and thick carpets
and am sad
that my grandfather
saw old age through
without scrawling love letters
addressed to dearheart
guiding him through the loss
of skin and vision

I touch my dead grandfather's
foot, he looks at me and smiles into
the golden stuff of ancestry in my forehead
his smile as kindly as the one or two
wrinkles swimming sideways from his eyelids

In real life, it is my father
who has cancer

In real life, my grandfather
died in a little boat
in the mossy ravines of Iowa
hunting the duck that my little boy
father would eat garnished with
wild apples, cooked slowly by
Mrs. Langly, served on a shiny
long maple brown table
with polished silverware

In real life, it is my father
who has cancer

and his little boy face
grew old so quickly
losing appetite for
the wild apples
and the duck so quickly

I dream that I eat his cancer
served on a long maple brown table
so that he can spend a Sunday morning
lying in bed thinking little boy thoughts
while the Iowa sun falls and plays in his
little boy room and while he plans what
little boy games he will play in the sun

I would eat your cancer
garnished with wild apples
and smile, chewing,
to give you one single morning of
infinite Sundays and boyish days
all made up of glad animal movements

You jerk out of bed this morning
with a tight grimace in the jaw
you grip the blankets and the pain
with your fists and your spine
it is Monday morning
and there is radiation to be had

You look at me, eyes little boy twinkles,
and smile into the golden stuff
of ancestry in my forehead
and I ask you how you feel
this morning

CANCER OF THE MOUTH

My sorrow
is sediment
and has settled
under the sand

I am trying to memorize the
planes and sockets
in your face that I
may still draw them
if you leave

You talk with commas
you talk the language
we speak with shopkeepers
bookkeepers, timekeepers
and with analysts

My sorrow cannot speak
your language, it cannot
be coined into your words

I am crying into my hands
my hands pressed up against
my eyebrows, twisting my face
into gnarled wood

I look up from the sculpture that
has become my face and you are
talking of provisions and of philosophy
you are looking at maps in your head

Maps of this body, this liver, an island,
taken, this alluvion, this blood, taken, all taken
by the cancer that we mouth and mouth

and talk around and around and
on top of and about and about
with prepositions, like acquisitions,
about your present condition

until we have cancer
of the mouth and of the heart

Sarah Ruhl *studies English and Classics at Brown University.*

"When the artist sits down to write, he makes himself."
—*Stephen Mallarmé.*

NATALIE SAFIR

WORDS FOR WHITE

You ask for a vocabulary of snow,
fresh words for the comfort of silence,
a drenching purity, the folding
and unfolding shawl that settles the land.

You read the snow for tracks,
sniff the freshened air
for grouse, roots rustling.

I study the sky, search bleakness
for the enchantment
that can reform scarred terrain.
Snow, I begin to see, has been
love for me through many winters.

In the drift of flakes, in the light
they hold, latinate words
are eased aside by branch, tall man,
brown dog, crunch and twig

falling lightly onto my page—
you, moving through northern fields.

Natalie Safir, who has published two collections, writes, edits and teaches poetry workshops by the Hudson River in New York.

ROBERT SAWYER

THE COUNTRY BOY

He was the first kid to sight
the silver planes pulling for the sun,

roaring full throttle to clear the heights
where clouds huddled like sheep afraid to run.
He knew he would fly those fragile machines
though he was stuck as an old fence stake
in mud where farms and barns and combines
rose as the highest summits.
He would not end in the Baptists' cemetery.
When it was his time, he'd lie in different
soil. Buenos Aires, he said, just to be contrary.
They said he was too smart for his own good, hard
as a mustang to break; soon he'd learn his place.
Then he left, came back a fighter ace.

Robert Sawyer, who holds down a job with the federal government and has a lively family, is completing a western novel set in the thirties.

"To use language well requires self-sacrifice, even giving up pet ideas." —Richard Hugo

DON SHEARN

THAW

The trucks from Streets and San
tear up the streets
"So they can save them."

A man huge belly,
magenta shirt
smokes a cigarette
steers a concrete cutter
through the road.

I am late for an appointment with a
guy named Chuck,
untrustworthy, and a slow payer.

My car breaks free from the pack.
I catch three lights in a row.

"He's not here. He went to lunch."
"It's 10:30."
"He got hungry."

I can't wait,
their paneling was eaten by spiders.
In the parking lot
early spring crawls through the vents in my suit.

Dogs jump through an opening in the fence.
The leader is a Lab-something mix,
sniffs the debris,
sorts out the raw from the cooked,
eats both.
A light rain begins,
tries to turn into sleet, but
lacks commitment.

I pull out;
the dogs in my rearview mirror
are moving on
too.

LUNCH IN CHINATOWN

Parking next to
       the projects
        (pale yellow stone
        green porches)
behind a Vega with its
           windshield smashed
           and patched
           with duct tape.

Rejection is a Dragon
invisible as myth.

THE SPRING TOUR: DUBUQUE

The town is dying.

On Main Street Mall
hand-lettered signs read
"for Lease."

A man lost in late middle age
and a T-shirt
fingers his baseball cap
flicks the ash off his cigarette.

In a bar with a big screen TV,
the businessman takes off his wedding ring
drinks a Margarita with more salt
than Tequila;
tells the waitress that he's staying
at the Comfort Inn,
that he stays up late,
that he's generous.

She laughs.
He's relieved and
drunk.

The road is a mirror, he tells himself,
when seen through the eyes of
a traveler.

Don Shearn has been writing poetry and fiction for 25 years and no longer worries about being ruined by early success.

"Don't get it right, get it written." —James Thurber

PEARL B. SHERIDAN

NOT ALWAYS AMBIVALENT

Okay, dammit, there's some things in life leave me undecided.
 To the fly I just killed in my kitchen, I apologize.
  Fair is fair, I reason with the corpse.
   I tried to shoo you out the door with a newspaper,
 But for once the <u>Wall Street Journal</u> was ineffective.

At two A.M. it's a feminist dilemma. Do I wake a sleeping husband?
   Admit cowardice? Lean on his sense of chivalry?
What about ethics? Swapping a dreamer for Jack the Ripper. . .
  "I need this?" he might protest, "At two A.M.?"
 But what if he hugs me, hands me some version of
"There, there, honey, don't you worry your pretty little head."
  Will my marriage survive past three A.M.?
   But with carpenter ants, no quarter to the enemy. I stand resolved.
   What are they doing in my home? Who sent for them?
All right, near the kitchen door. . .a short jaunt from the great outdoors.
   Curiosity, maybe. How are things by someone else?
  But in the upstairs bathroom. In the bedroom.
 In the study. They're planning to take a bath? Write a book?

 Bug sprays. . .Bad for the ecology. So call me unpatriotic.
I am spraying. My husband is spraying. Our son will soon be instructed:
"Spray! Don't just yell at them." Do they even have ears?
This war goes beyond all reason. Civilization is a thin veneer.

   What about the guilt? What about carpenter ants outside?
    I see them, climbing up the bricks, weaving little trails,
Leaving little messages, "This way to the clubhouse. Admission free."
    Twice, a large black ant has climbed up onto my knee.
     Was it a courier? An envoy from The Queen?
   Are they willing to negotiate? Who knows? I stamped on it.
     I am a killer.

TWO BOYS IN GRAY, TWO BOYS IN BLUE

Just a simple kind of day, is all it was,
Ma supervising washing in the tub,
Pa clearing out the stumps in the far field
Where we were going to plant a little cash crop,
Come next spring.

We didn't know it was a special day,
That last one, just before we had to leave,
Me setting out with Johnny, joining up.
Two men of honor riding with their regiment.
Two boys in gray.

No sun could shine as bright as Johnny's hair.
Pa used to joke they dipped him in a butter churn,
I always thought the story true. He didn't favor us.
Could have been hers, Aunt Betsy said.
Just lost his way.

When cousins Bart and Thomas came from Illinois,
We laughed to see how truly we were kin,
For there was Johnny's hair, sprouting on Bart,
and There was my own lanky form, carrying Tom.

Each summer, back and forth we visited each other,
Till we could spin a yarn as well as their Old Abe,
And they could jump their mount as well as any horseman
Here in Richmond. And folks would say we were the finest.
Cousins at play.

In time, Virginia went Confederate, and all of Illinois
Was for the Union. Jeff Davis chose his General Lee.
Abe Lincoln chose his General Grant. Johnny and I wore gray,
While Bart and Tom were turned out smart in uniforms of blue.
We had grown up.

We fought the Battle of Bull Run, where victory
Was ours. Wounded and dead lay stretched across the field.
As bugles sounded the retreat for Yankee troops,
My own sweet brother John laid down his head.

One sniper's bullet, John. Could you not dance away?
Sleep now, my Johnny Reb.

Step softly o the battlefields now covered
With green grass. And let their names be long remembered.
Antietam. And Gettysburg. Atlanta and Savannah. Richmond.
Their earth enfolds the soldiers who will not come home.
Rest now. Your work is done.

We lined the road, standing at sharp attention,
As General Lee, erect and proud, rode past his men,
Surrendering to Grant at Appomattox. No banners flew,
No band played Dixie, as we walked the long road home,
Never to leave behind the stench of dying horses,
The cries of wounded men.

Our skill with rifles was no longer needed.
Let others argue who was right, and who was wrong.
So we took off our gray and blue, leaving this history
For you to read and understand as best you can,
No longer lifting sword against a brother.
No longer struggling in "a house divided."

Pearl B. Sheridan is a teacher, editor and lecturer and published in anthologies as diverse as <u>Mother Poet</u>, <u>Blood to Remember, American Poets on the Holocaust</u>.

Chaim Nachman Bialik, Hebrew national poet, compared the prose writer to one who walked on layers of ice and the poet to one crossing a thawing river, leaping from one ice floe to another.

KAREN KOWALSKI SINGER

IT'S BEGINNING TO LOOK LIKE CHRISTMAS AT THE DINER

Early morning drizzle thickened up
into snow, slapping down like clumps
of wet oatmeal. Five days till Christmas,

people stamp into the diner,
shaking out their umbrellas, brushing
off their coats, saying, "NOW
it feels like Christmas!" Shirley
hums "Let it snow" while she hovers
around the overalled men who sit
draining cup after cup, teasing her:
"You want so much snow, honey,
you better start wearing your long johns."
"You mind your own underwear," she says.
Then she carts the pot around to fill
everybody up again. I let mine get cold
as I watch the sky shaking down
confectioner's sugar, while silverware
clinks in the kitchen like bells.

Karen Kowalski Singer, *of the Red Herring Poetry Workshop and Sangamon Poets, is a mother, a musician, and a dedicated journal writer.*

MARY WREN SMALL

GRANDMA

She had come from old Virginny,
her family connections not forgotten.
Uncomplicated, elegant,
she liked to dress up,
hated bunioned feet,
those cut-out shoes to keep her ambulant,
and being out of step, or obsolete.

Five children died—food scarce and misery abundant.
Grandpa was a preacher, left her cold—
divorce in nineteen hundred shocked the countryside.
Her life was full of memories, and she forgave.
But I remember how she sang to me—
"Oh Susanna"—softly, just a bit off key.

THE JOURNEY BACK

To journey back over crooked roads—
back to what we learned from our senses
and their mighty alphabet—
is part of the preparation
for our destined places,
like flowers plucked,
then dried and dropped
between the pages of a book—
slender lives fragile
now still, imprisoned
in a pocket of words.

ON BEING OLD

My thin and spotted arms hug life uncertainly.
I am engraved by time but not defeated
so I gather up the pieces of experience
with their transient effects and attempt
to make them sayable. I have still to
spend my restless fire although the dream
to be significant is fading fast.

To integrate it all is like an orchestra
of impulse, mind, and trivia of accidents, events,
their freighted consequence—a jagged way
to knowing, still forgetting much except,
perhaps, the vanished world of childhood,
a mother's touch, some cherished hours, and sorry
truths that mildew in the cellar of the mind.

We've stitched, unstitched the fabric of our lives.
Unlearning is the hard part, undoing harm
often to the dead to compensate
for hours unrecoverable, the ginger taste
of it both sweet and sour as we swallow
what we know about ourselves. It's an effort
to be sovereign over circumstance.

The task, almost religious, puts severed
parts together, sharpening our failures
into art, old glass shot through with winter's sun.

Mary Wren Small, born and educated in Ohio, nourished on poetry and classical literature, uses it to enrich her life with her three sons and three grandchildren.

"I think poetry is the pleasantest thing in the world and I like Henry James' insistence upon the felt life, as we collect who we are from the bale and bliss of it."

CHRISTINA SMITH

VISTA

The spurious blend of
evasive nights
floating in alcohol
and marinated
in the cool pan
of self-deception,
oh,
a few degrees centigrade
but
who's checking.
It gnaws,
this gloomy feeling
of want in the pit of night,
when nothing is subtle
but the lock on your door.
The creepiness grasps
behind your neck
like when you were punished
as a young girl
in your father's house

and he clutched you
by the scruff
so that a whole body
crumpled beneath
the crimson exhaust of your face.
It's not so simple now;
the air, dull and hot,
shifts testily
in chemical, alien waves
and no longer do you know
the fierce gentleness
of truth
or its sanding tool, devotion.
A fluid slide down,
what a slippery climb up,
unless you float
or take the stairs
to achieve a vista
at the top
of the chute.

Christina Smith *lives and works in San Francisco and is currently writing a novel.*

"When we get out of the glass bottles of our ego,/and when we escape like squirrels turning in the/cages of our personality/and get into the forests again,/ we shall shiver with cold and fright/ but things will happen to us/ so that we don't know ourselves."
—D. H. Lawrence

MICHAEL S. SMITH

JUMPING FOR JOY

Both boys roped in the other's eyes,
bouncing higher in their edgy corral
with each spring of the outlaw trampoline.

They circled as they bounced, flailed loose arms
as they sat down and stood up around
their conference table in the air,

negotiating for space and position,
competing to fly higher, to look down
on the other with a superior view.

It looked as dangerous as driving home
from work to me, as I watched them in stalled,
exhausted traffic; I ached to warn them

not to train for later confrontations,
when each move would only seem
spontaneous and such gaping-maw laughter
would hide turpitude or ambition.
This charming chaos and joyously awkward
ballet could fall like damned angels to earth.

They might no longer bounce up smiling
when they fall on their backs or help
their rival keep his place, jumping for joy,

and a misstep then, instead of breaking bones
or bloodying noses, could break hearts,
betray friends, or ground their soaring souls.

Michael Smith, a risk manager from Growmark, has published over one hundred poems, winning a number of national awards.

"A well-chosen anthology is like a long walk alone on a sunny beach."

MARILEE SNYDER

MIGRAINE LOVE POEM ABOVE A CONSTRUCTION SITE

I'm awake,   the left side of my head aflame,
this bed the scene of an arduous journey through night
a hurried encampment before dawn.

Sometime in the night they fired up the engines
of those earthmoving machines outside our window
and exiled me from the enchanted garden
scraping open,   just briefly,   the heavy earth laden with worms,
then leaving silence as wide as my eyes on through the dark and out
the other side.

I have lain here feeling my skin riot on the surface of my skull
as if the pain were a prairie fire ridden by wind
chasing rabbits and sage hens before it and
leaving behind it again and again the sparkling blackened ground.
I dare to touch you at this early hour
seeking something other than this prickling pain, this darkness,
something not included by the surveyed markers in the rutted dirt
where men will merely by laying sewer pipe.

In this silence bounded by pain and reverberation
I dare to soar like a nighthawk,   above the rim of your ear
trusting every breeze
laying my cheek so lightly against yours   you dream a distant cloud
You move warmly against me like canyons around a river
with the gentle authority that wears mountains down to sand
wildflower perfume rising hotly from the hissing sheets
and suddenly
A crow tears a hole through the treetops outside
dragging the unwilling sun behind her.
You smile,   your head turning,   eyelid opening only wide enough
to see straight through me   though softly
like the crow carrying the fine and perfect dawn on every feather.

Marilee Snyder is a Colorado backcountry-born, Northern California-alchemized, and Illinois-rooted woman, who tries to write as much poetry as possible and lives an otherwise decent life.

"...No one who survives/ to speak new language, has avoided this:/ the cutting-away of an old force that held her/ rooted to an old ground/the pitch of utter loneliness..." —*Adrienne Rich*

CAROL SPELIUS

POETS' ROUND ROBIN AT CONFERENCE

A circle of chairs wait, half-filled.
Poets file in, mostly women,
mostly grey-haired and wise. More
and more chairs line up, close ranks.
Coffee and ice water.

It is seven A.M. when we start to read.
The room sizzles with creative spirit.
The reader clutches his note-book,
his book of verse, or his memory,
not always dependable.
Like lightning, electric words
rampage: a baby born dead,
a father deserting his family,
a mother suicidal or violent,
the relentlessness of growing old,
declarations of undying love for Jesus.

Tender nerves, transformers
for tragedy and joy, ache
and vibrate. Flashes of humor,
welcome as spring rain,
lower the high voltage of pain.

After three days of circuit overload,
antennas withdraw. Protective shades
draw over eyes. We poets, forever
marked, go our separate ways.

In the empty meeting room, the magic
circle is gone. Untouched by poet
or poem, the chairs are now rearranged
at tables for lunch with the Elks.

Carol Spelius, *editor of Lake Shore Publishing, has a collection,
Gatherings, coming out in the fall.*

HEIDY ANNE STEIDLMAYER

THE HEALER
(for Ivan Cvetanovich)

It was the last thing I needed
to have this sick bird die
in my hands. It must have been the part
of me which always wished to fly
that held the ugly grackle
as if my touch could heal it.
In this town there's a Slovak healer
who cupped my hand like water
and slowly stroked the fingernails,
saying, you must learn to feel.
But these dead growths, dented
and bruised, descendants of claws,
feel the dull weight of his hand
but not his touch.

I hold in my hand a dead grackle, stiff
as a weathervane, which can not tell me
which way the wind blows or how to reach the sky.

Healing begins with the smallest touch,
to feel is to fly.

Heidy Anne Steidlmayer *says, "I write to right what isn't."*

"The best art unites the probable with the wonderful."
—Irving Babbitt

CAROLINE M. TONSOR

AUGUST

The sun says, "Stay!
Do not believe the end."
Who has not thought of Lot's wife
When the sun's decline
Poses the ultimatum, "Go!"
No, sinuous, more like the snake to Eve,
Promising fullness, ruinous, ripe,
Poised at the peak of its climb,
Ready to tumble down in shorter days,
In haze couched, in mist, diffused.

Grapevines tangle in the tree
And white grape sweetens under leaf.
Last apples darken in the noon,
Toughen to take the early dusk, the frost.

For whether it comes first to the marigolds
With their civet and ferret smell,
Or to the innocent fern,
Or to the manifold graceful grasses,
There will be frost.
There will be an end.

WATERDAYS

Small daughters wade, knee-deep,
The sandy laps of lakes.
Pebbles and vines of sunlight
Shimmer and trace
The shadows their stone-smooth bodies make.
Safe in the water's kindness
Plash and play.

In summer days
The year begins when all,

Impelled like water to go down,
Will skin the ledge and fall
And swim in lakes impounded
Like the summer days
Whose glitter and whose sunny surface hide
The drowned old stubblefields and trees.

I wear the day's dross, fear,
And swim unseen.
In underwater weeds I touch
A thousand pities, tangling.

Caroline Tonsor, educated, more or less, at the University of Illinois, has lived most of her life in Michigan with her historian husband, four children, and now grandchildren and all the materials of these poems every day.

"There lives the dearest freshness in deep down things..."
—Gerard Manley Hopkins

MEMYE CURTIS TUCKER

ANNA LEAVES HER RADIO ON

When you are out, Jean-Pierre Rampal
plays Telemann to keep burglars away,
better than you ever dreamed of playing.

All day, cadenzas trace your rugs,
eddy at the art glass, flow through the spines
of your first editions. How do I know this?

Once I happened to phone as you returned.
You said Hello, ran back to chain
the door, and flute notes poured through the line:

Birds, waterfalls—a breath part human,
part silver, supple as mercury,
as a thief in a room he knows.

RUBATO

Tonight again, the aging virtuoso
is taking liberties. His fingers slur,
almost forget. Yet the audience responds

to the sudden pianissimos, slow releases,
the thin body leaning into crescendos,
and Liszt's master trick—robbing

some notes, lingering on the ones he loves.
He's left behind the certain, dependable rhythms:
grandfather clock counting the nights of childhood,
the beat of his first metronome before its
broken weight began to slide, Pullman
wheels ticking the miles between concerts.

He gazes past the dark instrument, gathering
the times he has touched these phrases, playing now
in counterpoint to memory. He caresses, holds:
who doesn't long to mold tempo to shifting desire?

Memye Curtis Tucker's poems have appeared in a chapbook, <u>Holding Patterns</u>, in <u>Southern Review</u>, <u>Colorado Review</u>, <u>Cumberland Poetry Review</u>, and <u>Southern Poetry Review</u>; winner of the Georgia Poetry Circuit competition and the Armitage award and recipient of Individual Arts Grants from the Georgia Council for the Arts, she teaches the writing of poetry at the Callanwolde Arts Center in Atlanta.

ROD TULLIS

A DESTINATION

We drove past fields of thawing mud,
the bare oaks still covered with snow.
We drove through towns so small
and so silent that the shy wave
of the girl downtown on her bike,

who was in each of those towns,
was enough to welcome us.
Maybe, if we had chosen,
any of those towns could've served
as a destination, as a place to rest
the engine; but more, a place
where we might have lived a life
that we couldn't live anywhere else.
How much of our lives have we spent
in transit, between people, places,
things, even ideas of ourselves,
that we can commit to?
For whatever reason, as you finished
another beer and tossed the can
into the back of the truck,
as afternoon became evening,
as the fields around us grew rich
with expectation, we turned our backs
on each life as we created it.
Not even Breckenridge could stop us,
though we did slow through those buildings,
the wind's solo through broken
and boarded windows disturbed slightly
by the buzz of the car radio
we'd quit hearing hours before.
There was a simple park on the square,
or what at one time would've been
referred to as a park,
with long, brown, wind-blown grass
outlining the crumbling concrete
of what might've been a bandstand.
Its rusty top lopsided
and half fallen, a sculpture depicting
abstractly what no one needed to say.
Do we think we control change?
Is that why we go in search of it?

Rod Tullis, an ex-paratrooper, has published poems in such journals as <u>Black Warrior Review</u>, <u>Sycamore Review</u>, <u>Spoon River Poetry Review</u>, <u>Farmer's Market</u>, <u>Cincinnati Poetry Review</u>, and <u>Poetry Northwest</u>.

"Some people don't have the nerve to write bad poems, but I do."
—William Stafford.

CONSTANCE M. UTLEY

CHRISTMAS CARD

While the corn tassels waved pollen
Across the summer day you worked the
Green fields, plowing weeds under.
I watched your hay wagon on the
Dusty road, you passed with a nod.

At harvest time I left for
A city life.
Feeding pigeons on the roof top
I worried you would forget me.

At Thanksgiving you went to market
In Chicago with a truck load
Of fat steers—you didn't call me.
The pigeons called for crumbs
At my window.

There with you, snow covers black clods and
Cornstalks lean away from the wind.
Frost forms hexagons on wire fences
By mounds of steaming straw.

Here gray buildings grow tall.
Lonely people walk green and red
State Street smiling at plastic trees.

If you go to the seed store
By the train station, on Christmas Eve,
I may see you.

Constance Utley writes.

"Others betray the lamenting lies of their losses/ By the curve of the nude mouth or the laugh up the sleeve." —Dylan Thomas

WENDY WACKER

A MARRIAGE

My husband left my bones
on the Seder plate. The herbs
of renewal already chewed.

His brothers, my sisters
grin for the ritual. The gut,
the breath of our history

rounds the table. My daughter's
still wishful, untrained
in chant, her suffering secondhand

or something to come.
How did I get this old?

My husband rules the feast,
his stand-up routine,
while I watch the children,

try to hold it down,
watch the drooped clock,
its apathetic numbers.

Even the time is bored
by now. My halo's gone,
that nimbus of certainty—I understand

this life of mine—dropped
down with the sun
to a wild cloud

of storm. My son wides the door
and we wait for Elijah
who's supposed to break us

loose from this desert
bastille. The sand of vacation's
still moist in my shoes,

the wine in my blood
like the wind through the door
blows,

blows.
I might be an angel
ordained by marriage—

my own private Egypt.
I'll drift outdoors,
pass the prophet by,

sail to the beach
easy as mist,
as ritual smoke.

The sea's full of wind.
It blows.
It blows.

Wendy Wacker, *coming from a family of musicians, is proud to carry on in her own small way.*

"A poem is a very odd duck. It goes through changes—in form and color—when you leave it alone patiently, just as surely as a plant does, or an animal, or any other creature." —James Wright

CHERYL WALDSTEIN

LAST GIFTS

The family, still together that last time,
ate at Grandma's

sat at the table my father carried up three flights.
I climbed up slowly, in case the stairs caved in,
pretended I was sneaking, or just old.

In her room near the honey-colored bed
were glass bottles of gold perfume,
a picture of me on Grandpa's lap.
His hats and shoes in the hall closet still.
How scary nights alone must be,
trucks rumbling thunder,
a spider on the wall.

We made mandel bread in summer—
rolled out dough soft, as puffy as her wrists.
From the flour-dusted kitchen
we traced the zigzag of stairways up
and down the outside bricks.

My father swung me high into his convertible—
warm cookies sliding from the paper plate,
air sweetened with powdered sugar.
He blew the dust off and winked,
"We won't say a word."

We sang "Happy Birthday" that last time.
Grandma smiled with watery eyes and got the words wrong,
gave me a fluffy pink dress, bows pouring off the sleeves,
"Oh!" everyone said, as if watching fireworks
as my mother lowered it back into the box.
"A dress to save," she said and hid it.
I never knew where.

When it snowed, Grandma went to Miami.
I missed the soup I never ate,
its ladle melting back into the pot.
Magic flowers appeared on the white tablecloth,
glass and silver twinkling stars.
Rides home in pajamas past gray stairways like Grandma's,
I pretended to sleep, in the back of the car.
My parents fought about brisket and folding chairs.
I watched a secret show of moving shadows
on the vinyl screen, the back of my father's seat.

She sent me a plastic box of water and snow
to shake and make a storm—
reindeer and seashells and presents wrapped in bows.
My father said, "It's saltwater from the ocean."
And magic presents. The pink dress inside
the one on top. I know.

RUTH ROSE

No steam from the teapot rose
when Aunt Ruth forgot the water,
just a burnt metal smell
and a fireman
who carried her
in her yellow film of a nightgown,
to her "new home"—without a stove.

I took her cookbook.
Paper cover crackled,
browned and backless,
it rested in my still kitchen
near the cold soup pot.

Friday night,
waxy scent of candles lit,
lace tablecloth she had crocheted.
Ruth rose,
when I said by heart
the message from her book,
"Don't forget to give it,
once in a while, a little stir."

Cheryl Waldstein and her favorite critic specialize in raising lovely daughters (three) while she writes her new novel.

"The poet is an eternal door-opener while at the same time living with the sense of always being outside, of not being entirely at home even where he might be said to belong...Poetry is an entering into the lives of things and people, dreams and events, images and mindtides." —Brendan Kennelly

JUNE M. F. WILDEMAN

TO DRINK A STAR

We dipped into the silver spring
to drink a star of summer night
for all our lives' remembering.

How pure young love's companioning;
our groping thoughts of crystallite,
we dipped into the silver spring.

An owl on moonbeam-feathered wing
paused quietly in lucent flight,
for all our lives' remembering.

And what the foggy years should bring
or misty annals may indite,
we dipped into the silver spring.

The tender breeze began to sing
a ditty, juvenescent bright,
for all our lives' remembering.

To drink a star-illumined thing,
to hold the moment's depth and height,
we dipped into the silver spring
for all our lives' remembering.

WHEN I WAS A CHILD

The long leisurely journey of hours
form waking to unforeseen end of day
echoed eternity.
Carefree, I wandered a fresh world
in the meadows of morning.
Love fed my eyes with discovery
well before mid-day meal.

After the high sun,
in the newness of afternoon,
everywhere waited a turning of surprise.
When the sleepy lavender of evening
enfolded me, blurring the bird calls,
I lay down, beloved and secure,
observed by the also curious stars.

June M. F. Wildeman is an itinerant poet, teacher, wife, mother, religious and secular volunteer, and insurance broker.

"(Poetry) should strike the reader as a wording of his own highest thoughts, and appear almost as a remembrance." —John Keats

RICHARD ZABRANSKY

THE NIGHT FATHER CRIED

She wanted to read about missionaries,
a book thick with God,
but sixty watts kept him from a world
where rattlesnakes brought
a dollar-a-head,

and eight hours of drafting blueprints
dissolved like indigo
in the cold stream
that cut the walls
of Immigration Canyon.

But neither counting backwards
from a thousand, nor puffing like a frog
could get him past the state line:
the bridge was washed out
by a purposeful glow.

His house slipper settled it:
the vacuum popped.
In the electric dark
she opened the dresser drawer,
flinging sparks from flannel,

spewing a censar of Chanel.
She loaded the overnight
with handfuls of hurt,
took her flashlight for flipping the page,
and creaked a firm exit.

She made it to the backyard trellis,
sat vined in the moonlight
while truckers in the business of America
exchanged beams on highways
father had mapped.

DOLLS

They were kicked aside
to clear the stairway.
Their plastic baby faces
glow of being loved,
like Mrs. Laurie's cat.
Norm Carlson swears at them
for getting in his way
when he carries groceries up.
There must be thirty of them
and at night
glassy eyes follow me to the door.

Pass them silently,
careful to avoid their eyes.
There is an effort
to walk on the other side of the stairs,
in single file,
at least until
a decision is reached.

The lightbulb at the top of the stairway
is beginning to flicker.
Mr. Frietag leaves down the fire escape;
Mrs. Frietag stays home.
Norm Carlson broke his leg.
Mrs. Laurie's cat died.
At least one family has begun to pack.
We are at a point
where it seems something must be done.
As the last resort,
we are thinking of asking
the children for help.

MY WIFE'S COUSIN MARY CALLS FROM THE BRONX

From just beyond the neck of the Hudson,
touched by the shadow of St. Theresa's spire,
Mary calls. The wires must be worn,
an angry static stretch the line:
boney as vertebrae, the connection threatens to break.

The world's in paralysis
in her Irish enclave.
On the shelf below the Korean grocer's cash drawer,
bullets nudge from silos.
Westchester Avenue is stained with tinted glass
from blackened windshields that spider-webbed.
The whitewash flakes from Yankee walls.

But Fran has had a baby, Kevin James,
his cry challenges the horns out on the sound.
Would I give Kathleen the news when she returns?
Mary's vowels clog my Midwest ear,
her ow's and oooh's swell
like the <u>Tribune</u> left out in the rain:
section by section the words bleed through.

But, I'm good at messages,
have a knack for getting down the drift,
and, when I pass it on, I get dry cleaning in exchange:

my starched cotton oxford white as bone,
a tweed sports coat minus the banquet stain,
safe inside their filmy sacs.

My wife runs to the phone, is thrilled:
her bloodline grows.
A new pair of eyes squint through a dim Atlantic haze
as from the backyards of my suburban sprawl,
fleshy drippings flare on hot coals.

Richard Zabransky, a writing instructor, received an M.A. from San Francisco State University.

Reading Hart Crane's line "the seal's wide spindrift gaze toward paradise," taught me that a poetic image can disclose entire worlds.

THORNTREE PRESS LIBRARY

THE LITERATURE PERSON'S
GUIDE TO NAMING A CAT
       $5.95
  by Lawrence Jarchow

LOOKING ACROSS $7.95
  by Marcia Lee Masters

TROIKA I $5.95
The Accident of Light
  by Marilyn Taylor
Blue Depression Glass
  by Barbara Unger
Children of the Glassblower
  by Debra Kay Vest

TROIKA II $5.95
Giving Death the Raspberries
  by Carol I. Gloor
Saving Up the World
  by Janice Lynch
Tattoo
  by Gregg Shapiro

WILD THINGS IN THE YARD
       $5.95
  by Wendy Anderson

YOU ARE INVOLVED IN
A FABLE $5.95
  by Barry Goodman

WAVING AT TRAINS $5.95
  by John Dickson

GIRL IN THE EMPTY
NIGHTGOWN $5.95
  by Eloise Bradley Fink

THE DISAPPEARANCE OF
GARGOYLES $5.95
  by Mary Makofske

WHAT IS GOOD $5.95
  by Hilda Raz

WHEN THE PLOW CUTS
       $5.95
  by Katie Andraski

NAMING THE ISLAND $5.95
  by Judith Neeld

TROIKA III $5.95
Color Documentary
  by LuAnn Keener
Kitchen of Your Dreams
  by Katharyn H. Machan
Side Effects of Life
  by Laura Telford

TROIKA IV $5.95
Funny How You Remember
  by Judy Brinkworth
Pulling Up the Dawn
  by Helen Reed
Hidden Seed
  by Laurel Mills

TROIKA V $5.95
Don't Ask Why
  by Glen Brown
File Under Melancholy
  Martin Marcus
Lithic Scatter
  Lydia Webster

**Shipping and Handling
per book** $2.00

Gathered from California to Connecticut, Minnesota to Mississippi, here is your <u>Neighborhood of Poems.</u> We hope you'll move into those pages where you feel most at home. Visit with the other poems until they seem friendly.

Some, of course, are easy to know, although others are more aloof and may summer at the shore or live in a city far away from your experience. They may speak to you today—or next year. Neighborliness can be a surprise.

Some readers see poetry as a ticket to everywhere—even tomorrow. Others consider it therapy—take two poems and call me in the morning. Yet others think of it as a business of collecting enough poems to jingle in the pocket. Whoever you may be, we think you'll find the poems friendly enough to live next door.

Mostly, we hope you'll remember you're always welcome here. You may, of course, bring your own poems along if you like; or, just for the metaphor of it, send us a photocopy of one to be enjoyed as a kind of poemgranate under the Thorntree. Although we are not able to write to you, we'll read you and like being in *your* neighborhood.

Eloise Bradley Fink

9

13

14

16

18

19

22

26

27

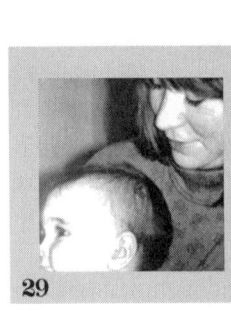

29

30

35

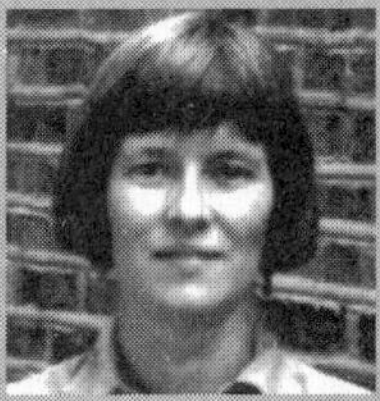
37

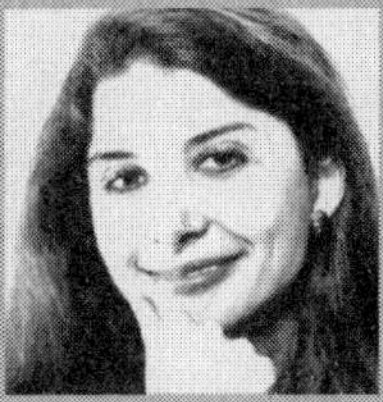
40

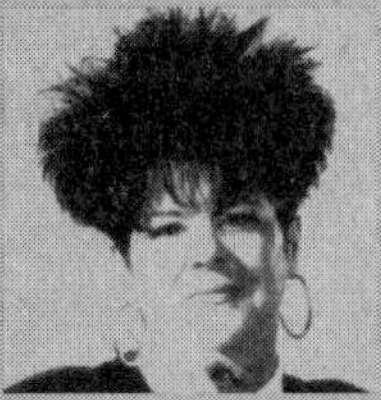
42

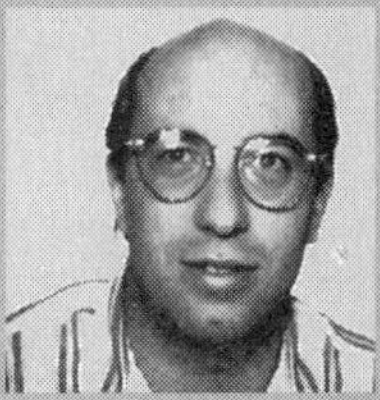
46

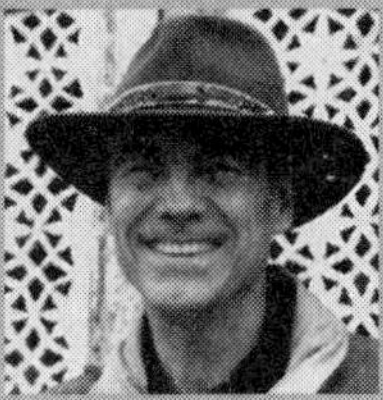
48

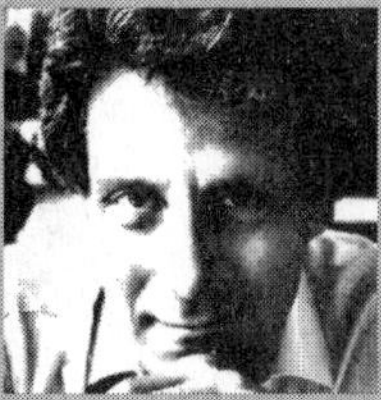
51

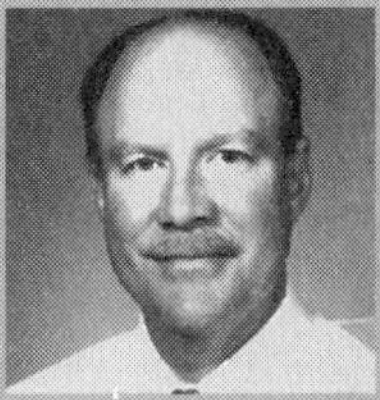
53

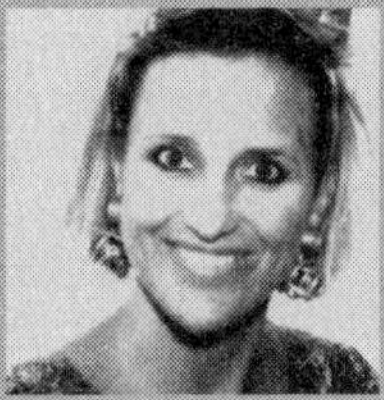
54

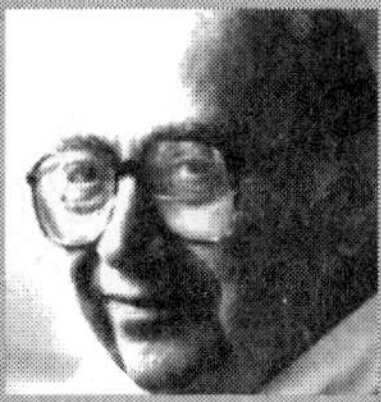
56

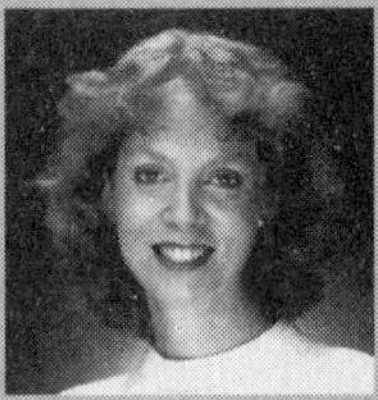
59

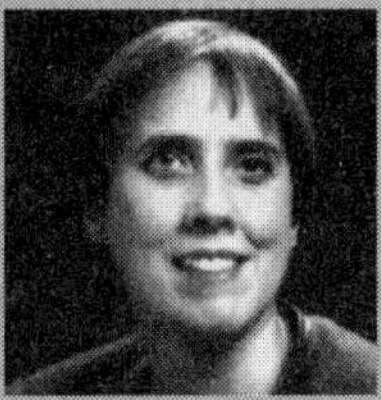
60

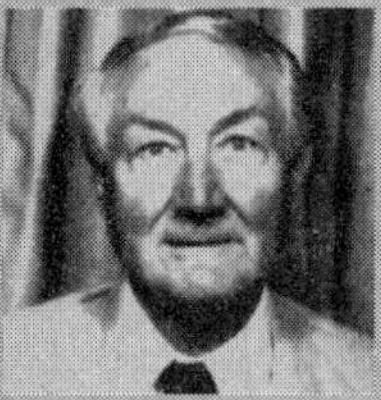
61

62

64

66

67

67

68

69

73

74

74

76

78

79

81

81

83

86

88

89

90

92

94

95

97

99

102

108

109

114

116

118

123

123

124

127

129

130

132

133

135

136

137

138

139

140

142

143

144

147

148